ONE HUNDRED PLUS

DECK
DESIGNS

SINGLE-LEVEL DECKS • MULTI-LEVEL DECKS
L-SHAPED DECKS • AND MANY MORE!

HOME PLANNERS, LLC
Wholly owned by Hanley-Wood, Inc.
Tucson, Arizona

International Standard Book Number: 1-881955-90-7
Library of Congress Catalog Card Number: 2001088993

Home Planners, LLC
Wholly owned by Hanley-Wood, LLC
Tucson, Arizona 85741

10 9 8 7 6 5 4 3 2 1

Book design by Jay C. Walsh and Teralyn Morriss.
Edited by Morenci Wodraska, Jennifer Lowry and Paulette Dague.

Front and back cover photos courtesy of Louisiana-Pacific Corporation.

CONTENTS

A deck addition complements your home in delightful ways and enhances your lifestyle by adding an essential outdoor "room." If you're considering a deck for your home, you'll be wise to investigate the choices you have for decking and railing materials. There are more options than traditional wood decking—

ALL DECKED

options that make better sense and are equally as attractive. By using the latest composite decking and railing materials, you'll create an outdoor area that is environmentally friendly, easy to install and virtually maintenance-free.

Photos courtesy of Decks USA

OUT

THE LIFESTYLE OF DECKS

Hosting a garden party, taking a nap with a cool spring breeze wafting over you, watching birds and squirrels scampering in the yard. You can make the daydream of outdoor enjoyment and relaxation a reality if you plan the perfect spot to do all of these things and more. Outdoor spaces—patios, porches, balconies, decks—are practically necessity items for today's well appointed home. Among them, decks are by far the most popular because of their rustic charm and casual good looks. Blending perfectly with natural surroundings, decks unite your home with your landscape in ways that hard, cold concrete could not begin to do. And decks allow more flexibility and can easily be made larger than either porches or balconies.

Examine the possibilities with a deck addition:

- *Adds outdoor space to expand a living or dining area*
- *Creates a focal point for landscaping and gardening*
- *Opens a small interior space visually*
- *Provides safe play space for children*
- *Offers a relaxing area for reading and conversing*
- *Allows an outdoor "kitchen" with the addition of a barbecue*
- *Increases the usability and appeal of your home, including boosting its resale value*

PLAN THE PERFECT DECK

With a bit of planning and the right materials, a deck addition can become the favored spot in your yard—and can be easily maintained for many years. Consider the advantages of composite decking and railing material.

What Is Composite Decking?

Composite decking is a manufactured material, composed of recycled and/or excess wood products and plastic. It is designed to better withstand weather conditions than traditional wood decking and offers low-maintenance good looks for years. The WeatherBest™ line of composite decking and railing is manufactured by Louisiana-Pacific, a major building products company headquartered in Portland, Oregon.

WeatherBest™ decking comes with an attractive wood-grain finish. When newly installed it looks like new wood planks, but

gradually weathers over time to a soft ivory-gray, depending on regional weather conditions.

WeatherBest™ decking is available in 5⁄4" x 6" solid and 2" x 6" hollow planks, either of which may be used for deck surfaces, porches, walkways and boat docks. Though it is not required, pre-drilling will provide a more attractive finish, plus you'll use standard tools for installation.

Railing components from Weather-Best™ come in 2" x 6" top rails, 2" x 4" side rails and 2" x 2" balusters and may be used around

decks or porches, and on walkways and boat docks. These components also install with standard tools. Railings and components are sturdy and strong and easily attach to your deck, porch, walkway or boat dock.

The Advantages of WeatherBest™ Composite Decking and Railing

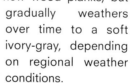

Composite Decking & Railing

Composite Decking and Railing is a natural-looking choice around pools and spas and blends beautifully with other landscaping features.

Sturdy, Yet Natural-looking

The WeatherBest™ line of composite decking by Louisiana-Pacific cuts, drills and fastens similar to wood, but unlike wood it resists cracking, splintering and checking. In addition, it's resistant to termites, rot and decay, making it the ideal choice in termite-prone areas and coastal, lakeside and pool applications. Because it is a manufactured product, the decking and railing materials are straight and true, never twisted or crooked as traditional wood decking can be. Its smooth surface contains no splinters or knots.

Low-Maintenance Choice

Unlike traditional wood decking materials, WeatherBest™ Composite Decking and Railing won't require staining, sealing, painting or expensive treatments. However, if you decide you'd prefer a painted or stained appearance, you may apply non-opaque oil-based stains after the boards are fully weathered.

Routine maintenance chores are at a minimum. Use a flat tool, when necessary, to clean out the expansion gaps between the boards to ensure proper drainage. Normal cleaning is easily accomplished using a common deck cleaner.

Safe for Children and Pool Areas

WeatherBest™ Composite Decking and Railing is splinter-free, so children can play freely on the decking surface without harm. Adults have the comfort of knowing that they can walk barefoot on the decking surface—a plus around pools—with carefree assurance.

Environmentally Friendly

Because it is made of recycled materials and excess wood products, Weather-Best™ com-

posite decking and railing is kind to the Earth's environment. And since it requires no paint, stain or sealant, you'll never have to worry about harsh or dangerous chemicals leaching into your yard or ground water.

Creative Option for Landscaping

The natural beauty and woodsy charm of WeatherBest™ composite decking and railing make it suitable for even the most elaborate landscaping scheme. It blends perfectly with natural environments and is much easier to maintain than traditional wood products. With an attractive appearance and fewer maintenance headaches, WeatherBest™ products are a landscaper's dream.

DECK BUILDING BASICS

Building a deck is not complicated, if you have the proper tools and a little knowledge about the basics of construction. Following are some tips on building decks in general and using WeatherBest™ composite decking and railing to get you started in the right direction.

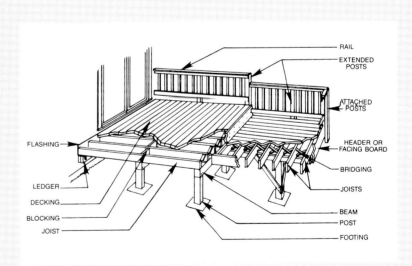

Parts of a Deck

Here is a basic deck structure that can be used for almost any deck. It consists of posts, beams and joists, which support the decking and railing. Also shown are the additional details that make up the deck's structure.

GLOSSARY OF DECK-BUILDING TERMS

Beams — Lateral support lumber members that are attached to posts. Joists rest on top of the beams.

Blocking — Boards the same dimension as the joists, placed between the joists to supply additional support.

Bracing — Part of the substructure, required when decks are four feet or more above ground. Braces are attached to posts to prevent lateral movement.

Decking — The actual deck surface. Deck boards are attached to the joists. Decking is available in a number of different kinds of wood and composite materials.

Flashing — Metal material that angles over the ledger board to protect it and to prevent moisture from accumulating on the ledger and against the house wall.

Footings — Supports often made of concrete that are positioned on or in the ground. Footings must rest on firm soil so the deck support system will not shift or sink.

Header — Also termed facing board, a length of lumber that attaches to the outside of the deck.

Joists — Lateral support boards that are attached to (or lay on top of) beams. Decking boards are attached to the joists.

Ledger board or Ledger plate — A board that is attached to the house usually bolted to the floor joist. This allows the house to support one side of the deck.

Piers — Attached to footings and used to support the deck posts. Often made of concrete. Posts are often attached to piers.

Posts — The upright support lumber members that are attached to piers and footings. Posts extending above deck level can also serve as railing supports.

Riser — A term used with stair construction. The vertical distance the step rises from one step to the next. Also, the board that creates the rise.

Setback distances — The distance from the property line to the deck.

Splicing — When the length of deck span prevents beams or joists from reaching the complete distance, splicing involves placing two lengths of wood together to complete the distance. It is best to splice beams at the posts for the strongest connection.

Toenailing — Nailing two boards together with nails driven into boards at an angle. The fastest but least effective method of joining boards.

Tread — A term used with stair construction. Refers to the surface or surface board that is walked on.

Selecting a Site

Where you build your deck depends on several factors. Often the orientation of your home and available outdoor space narrow your options, and placement is obvious. If you have several site choices, spend some time thinking about them. Building a deck is similar to building a room—what will be its primary purpose? As a common rule of thumb, a deck will perform the same function as an adjoining indoor room. For example, a deck adjacent to the kitchen becomes a place for meals or a barbecue site. A deck off the master bedroom could be used for relaxation or a sunny spot to read the Sunday paper. Thinking about how your family will use the deck is valuable in determining its size, shape and location.

A Design for Comfort

Climate, and the many small climates in and around your lot called microclimates, deserve special consideration. A poorly positioned deck, climate-wise, could jeopardize your outdoor comfort, making the deck area unlivable many days of the year. Note the direction of prevailing breezes. Do you want exposure to cooling breezes, or shelter from blustery winds? Living with the sun is a similar love-hate relationship. In cold northern climates and dur-

SURVEY TO OBTAIN A TRUE CORNER

A simple surveying procedure allows you to be sure your deck will be built square, with true 90-degree angles. The goal of the survey is to construct a right triangle to be sure deck corners will be built square. This is the "3-4-5 method" or the "6-8-10" method.

The 3-4-5 method. Using stakes and string, run a line (Line One) parallel to house or wall that deck will be against. If deck is freestanding, pick any edge of the proposed deck to use as the base line. Drive a stake near the end of Line One and attach a second line (Line Two.) Run Line Two perpendicular to Line One several feet long. Use a length of string or tape measure and measure 4 feet in length along base line. Attach another line 3 feet long or use a tape measure to measure from the stake along Line Two. Measure the distance across from Line Two and Line One. The corner is exactly square when this distance equals 5 feet. Use a carpenter's square in the corner to double-check your accuracy.

ing certain times of the year, a sunbathed deck is a blessing, whereas in the warm southern climates, afternoon shade is almost always required during summer months. To determine shading and sun requirements, note sunrise and sunset patterns and how shade from structures and trees falls on your proposed deck site. Be aware that sunshine and shade patterns are seasonal. The summer sun is high in the sky and shines for a longer period; thus shadow patterns are different than in winter, when the sun is lower in the sky and shines for a shorter time. Designing combination sun/shade locations for the deck for different seasons is ideal.

Deck Layout

Creating a site plan is common when developing a plan for a home landscape. It is an exercise that works well with deck layout and placement, as well. A site plan allows you to sketch out on paper existing features—property lines, utility lines, permanent mature plants, land contours, buildings, roads, views to preserve and views to conceal. All of this helps to figure placement of the deck, landscape plans and other outdoor features. After you've recorded these, you can then note smaller, less important items.

Some designers use overlays of tracing paper for different elements: one for plants, one for ground surface materials, one for built-up structures and so on. Other overlays could include utility poles and underground utility lines, neighboring buildings, driveways, walkways and even bothersome noises.

Permits and Codes

Building Permits. Before you purchase materials or begin building, be sure you have all building permits. If your deck includes any electrical work, such as lighting on stairways, or plumbing, such as a food preparation sink, you'll need permits for each of these.

TOOLS CHECKLIST

Building a deck does not require a lot of specialized tools—this is true of both natural wood decks and composite decks. Those required are usually found in the average handyman's garage. Gathering the tools you need before you begin construction is as important as having the building materials in sufficient supply and quantity. If you don't want to purchase all of these, many are available at rental shops.

- **Carpenter's level**
- **Chalk line**
- **Chisel**
- **Hammer**
- **Handsaw**
- **Line level**
- **Nail set**
- **Plumb bob**
- **Portable power circular saw**
- **Portable power drill**
- **Portable power jigsaw**
- **Shovel**
- **Tape measure** (100 foot)
- **Tool belt**
- **Wheelbarrow** (handy to move stuff and to mix concrete for footings, etc.)

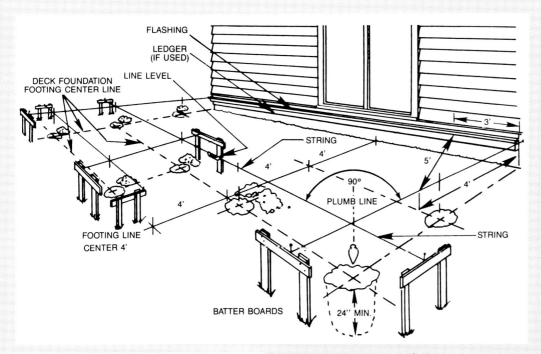

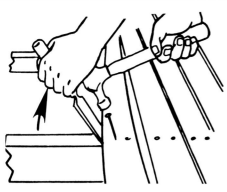

Locating Footings and Piers
Using batter boards to hold string tight and level, locate the center of all footings with a plumb line. Depth of footings depends on local codes, but at least 6 inches below frost line is recommended. Make sure the string is square by using the 3-4-5 triangle method as shown. See text for complete explanation.

Deck Tools: Most are Basic
Most deck construction requires using common hand tools such as a hammer and chisel, in this instance used in combination to straighten a board with an outward bow.

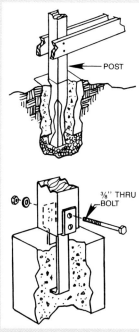

Attaching Support Posts to Footings and Piers

Above: A below-grade post and footing connection. Post is set in concrete and beams are attached with nails. This is a quick and simple method, but not the strongest.

Below: A step-flange anchor uses steel angles set in poured concrete, and post is secured with bolts and washers. This kind of method creates a strong connection that is less susceptible to wood rot.

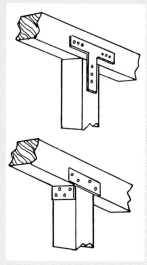

Post to Beam Connections

Two methods of attaching posts to beams: a T-strap and metal flange and notched beam connection. Select a method that will be strong and long lasting to help ensure the life and safety of your deck.

Building Codes. Equally important is constructing the deck to meet local codes, usually imposed by city or county governments. Codes are required to be sure your deck meets minimum standards for safety and construction methods. In addition, neighborhood and zoning regulations may exist. Check also with nearby neighbors about your plans to build.

Site Drainage

Drainage is an important word to remember when beginning deck construction. Water must drain away or it will pool on structural supports, eventually rotting and weakening them. The easiest way to supply drainage is to slope the ground away from home and deck so water will run off naturally. If the ground does not slope naturally, you can dig a drainage channel or channels to carry water away.

STRUCTURAL ELEMENTS

Note: WeatherBest™ decking is not for use as a structural element. Consult with state and local authorities in your area, or your builder for codes and regulations regarding structural members, beams, studs, columns and stringers.

Installing Footings and Piers

Footings and piers create the foundation, holding the deck's support posts in place. Weak footings can ruin even the best-constructed deck. Local codes vary as to correct footing and pier sizes and depths. If you are in a region where the ground freezes, footings are placed a code-recommended depth below the soil level. Find out before digging. Always call your local utility to identify pipeline and cable locations before you dig.

Attaching Support Posts to Footings and Piers

The size and number of posts are determined by the size of the deck, and the weight it will be required to support. Posts that are 4x4-size are normally suitable for an average deck. If the deck is 6 feet or more above ground, or will be required to support heavy loads, use 6x6-size posts.

There are a number of ways to attach the posts to the footing and piers. Two common methods are shown in the illustrations at left. Check local codes to determine which methods are acceptable.

Attaching Posts to Beams

The illustrations at left show two common methods of attaching beams, also called stringers, to the posts. Install these after the first row of posts has been set in place. Bolting beams to posts with quality, galvanized connectors is the strongest method, and recommended.

Attaching Joists to Beams

Joists are attached to the beams to serve as the support for the actual decking boards. Be sure they are cut the correct size. If cut too long, they tend to bow if forced into place. Two methods of attaching are shown on the next page. If you decide to toenail the joist to the beam, be careful to avoid splitting the joist, which could weaken the structure. Blunting nails before pounding them into the wood helps avoid splitting the joist.

Structural Bracing

Decks that exceed four feet high from ground level require that posts be braced to resist lateral movement. Normally, bracing is required only around the deck's perimeter, but it must be continuous.

Use 2x6 lumber for all braces, and attach to posts with two bolts in each end. Use washers with bolts to help prevent gouging and resulting decay of the wood.

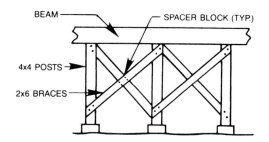

Structural Bracing

Several designs can be used for substructure bracing, recommended for decks over four feet high. Shown is "X" bracing design.

LAYING THE DECK SURFACE

When laying the decking, start at one end, squaring the first board with the header. As you nail boards, measure as you go to be sure boards are being nailed straight. Note: Construct stairways before nailing down decking. A predetermined nailing pattern will secure the decking well and give the surface a more professional, finished appearance. Weather-Best™ Composite Decking and Railing is available in two product configurations (5/4" x 6" solid WeatherBest[SP] and 2" x 6" hollow planks WeatherBest[EHP]), which have different joist spacing. It is advised that you decide on a finishing method (there are three options) when using WeatherBest[EHP] hollow deck boards, to ensure that the substructure will accommodate it.

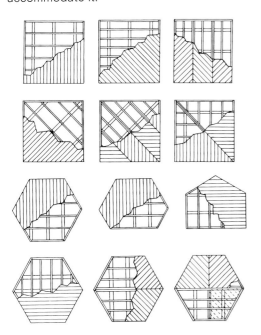

Deck Shapes and Surface Patterns

A selection of rectangular and octagonal framing plans shows several deck shapes and surface patterns. Note the different designs of the substructures. Select and build a substructure that will accommodate the deck surface pattern you want.

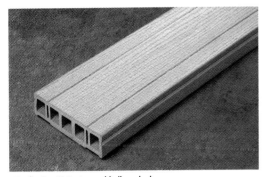

WeatherBest[EHP] Engineered hollow planks.

Installing 2" x 6" Hollow WeatherBest[EHP] Decking

The hollow 2" x 6" decking boards are intended to be installed on joists up to 24 inches on center. Traditional fasteners (galvanized or stainless steel nails or deck screws) will work well. Hidden fastening is also an option.

A minimum of ⅛" spacing between boards and ¼" at the ends is usually sufficient to allow for expansion during temperature changes and for drainage of water or melting snow and ice.

The edges of hollow WeatherBest[EHP] composite decking may be finished in one of three ways (and, as mentioned above, it is best to determine which you'll use ahead of time):

- **Edge Skirting:** When all boards are fas-

tened, use a chalk line across the overhanging boards and trim any excess boards. Use WeatherBest[EHP] planks, cut to the necessary length and fastened to the rim joist. The edge skirting will cover the hollow ends of the boards.

- **Framing:** Attach deck boards around the perimeter of the deck frame, mitering the ends to close off the hollow sections. (Be sure there are support joists located properly underneath the framing boards.) Then apply deck boards between the framing.

- **Universal Cap:** After all the deck boards have been installed, use a chalk line across the overhanging boards and trim any excess boards. After trimming, attach WeatherBest™ Universal Caps to the end of the deck boards by screwing from underneath the decking.

WeatherBest[SP] Solid Planks.

Installing ⅝" Solid WeatherBest[SP] Decking

The solid WeatherBest[SP] ⅝" x 6" decking boards are intended to be installed on joists spaced up to 16 inches on center. Reduce spacing by four inches when applying boards diagonally. Traditional fasteners (galvanized or stainless steel nails or deck screws) will work well. When applying screws, the wood fibers may mushroom out from the hole. Simply hammer this lightly to cover the deck screw. Although not required, pre-drilling the holes will eliminate the mushrooming and provide a cleaner, more attractive installation and is highly recommended. Many commercially available hidden fastener systems will work well with WeatherBest[SP] solid decking. Check manufacturer's recommendations for specific installation for composite decking material.

A minimum of ⅛" spacing between boards and ¼" at the ends is usually sufficient to allow for expansion during temperature changes and for drainage of water or melting snow and ice.

When all of the boards have been installed, use a chalk line across the overhanging boards and trim any excess boards. After

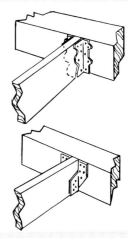

Attaching Joists to Beams

Framing anchor, above and hurricane anchor, below, are two common methods of attaching joists to beams. Joists become the supports for the actual decking boards. Use metal joist hangers such as these on joists located between beams.

being trimmed, the composite boards will have a smooth finish and need no additional sanding or finishing. The boards should not hang more than 2 inches over the rim joist.

RAILINGS

In most areas, decks over three-feet-high require a railing. The generally specified height of the railing is also three feet. Railings are integral to the safety of your deck, so local building codes should be reviewed carefully before beginning construction.

WeatherBest™ composite railing components come in 2 x 6 top rails, 2 x 4 side rails and 2 x 2 balusters. The components cut, drill and install similar to wood.

Note: WeatherBest™ railing should not be used as a structural component. Consult with local or state authorities in your area regarding building codes and regulations for structural members, joists, beams, studs, columns and stringers.

STAIRS AND STEPS

Stairs and steps are extensions of deck design—allowing you to connect decks of varying levels, or providing exits to ground level. Stairs are composed of the tread, the riser and stringers (the supports on which the steps are attached). Stairs are usually 4, 5 or 6 feet wide and must be built carefully with a constant riser-to-tread ratio. A common deck

ratio is 6:12, meaning, if the tread is 12 inches the next step should rise 6 inches. Steps can also be constructed as a single step from deck to ground or from one deck level to another. Some steps are constructed as a separate level, a kind of continuous step, from one deck to another. The illustration below shows the options for stringers and treads, plus a chart indicating standard tread-riser ratios.

THE WEATHERBEST™ WARRANTY

WeatherBest™ Composite Decking and Railing is warranted against checking, rot, decay and termite damage for a full ten years. The warranty is fully transferable should you sell your home while coverage is in effect.

CHOOSING A DECK PLAN

Following this section is a special collection of 127 deck designs, from wonderfully simple to elegantly elaborate. Each has been custom created for use with WeatherBest™ composite decking and railing. Take some time to browse through these plans to find the one that is perfect for your home and family. Then turn to page 140 for information about ordering a complete set of deck plans that will allow you to get started on your own special outdoor space.

TREAD
WOOD CLEATS
4x4 IN CONCRETE BOLTED TO STRINGER

Basic Step Designs

Above Right: With open-riser design steps, treads are attached to wood or metal cleats that are secured to stringers.

Below Right: Closed-riser design steps feature stringers that are notched to support tread risers for a stronger, more finished design.

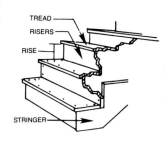

TREAD
RISERS
RISE
STRINGER

STRINGER AND TREAD OPTIONS

STANDARD TREAD-RISER RATIOS	
Tread Width	Riser Height
11"	6½"
12"	6"
13"	5½"
14"	5"
15"	4½"
16"	4"

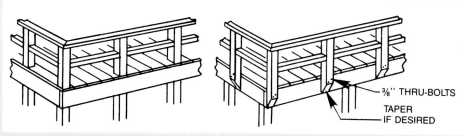

⅜" THRU-BOLTS
TAPER IF DESIRED

Railing Design

Above Left: Some deck designs allow support posts to be extended, serving as railing supports.
Above Right: Alternate design shows how rail posts can be bolted to facing to provide support.

Design HPU050001
Square Footage: 226
Width: 20'-0" Depth: 14'-0"

*T*his deck plan offers box steps to the yard, a floating bench and inter-
esting angles. A wide stair provides interaction with the yard beyond,
yet keeps a more formal space for entertaining or dining needs.

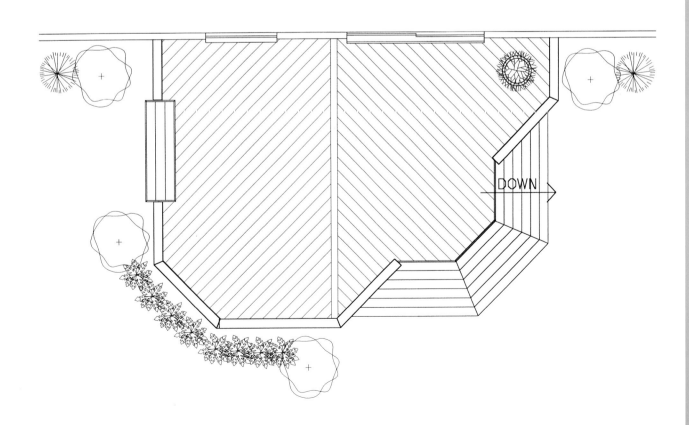

Design HPU050002

Square Footage: 259
Width: 20'-0" Depth: 13'-6"

*D*ouble-decker appeal! A long staircase leads to the lower deck, which features a wrapping, floating bench to accommodate extra guests or relaxing. The upper level is a prime spot to look out onto the yard or enjoy the view of the night sky.

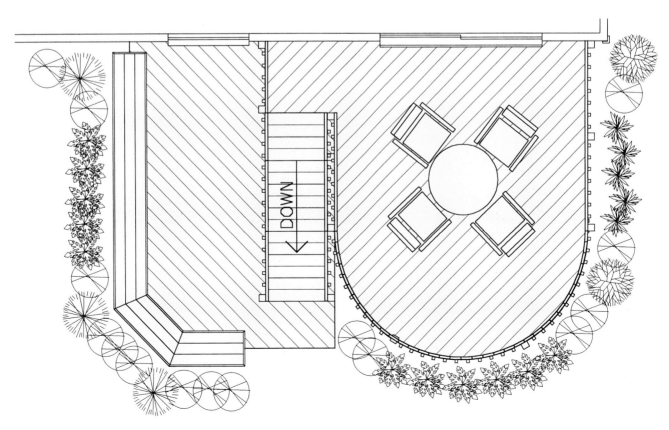

DOWN

Photo courtesy of ©Decks USA, Inc.

This home, as shown in the photograph, may differ from the actual blueprints. For more detailed information, please check the floor plans carefully.

Design HPU050003
Square Footage: 240
Width: 21'-0" Depth: 13'-0"

*T*his design is a multi-level delight with an overlook platform just outside your door. A step up features a floating bench, another bench flanked by large planters and access to a flight of stairs that lead to the yard below.

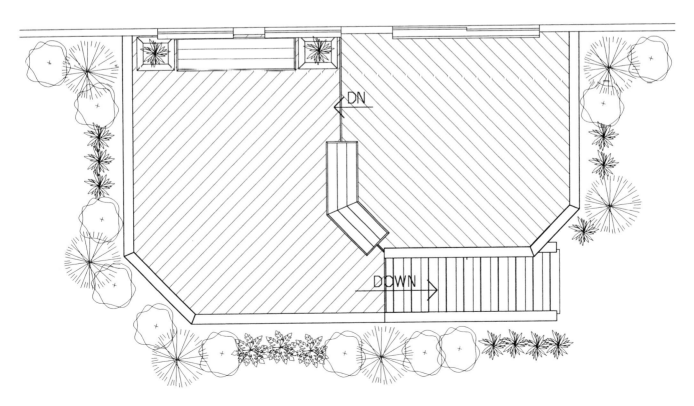

DN

DOWN

Photo courtesy of ©Decks USA, Inc.

This home, as shown in the photograph, may differ from the actual blueprints. For more detailed information, please check the floor plans carefully.

Design HPU050004

Square Footage: 271
Width: 20'-0" Depth: 14'-0"

*A*n open platform arrangement offers unobstructed views and interac-tion with nature. Floating benches offer comfort and a place to sit and wile away the afternoon. Twin stairways on opposite sides of the deck and a long central stair make it easy to reach the yard beyond.

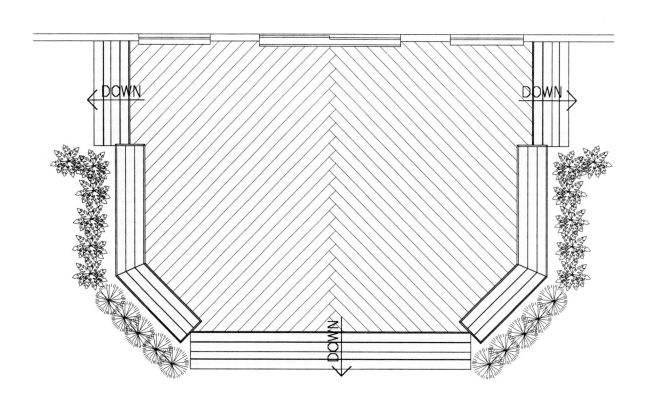

Design HPU050005
Square Footage: 281
Width: 25'-0" Depth: 15'-0"

*S*tep out to enjoy a great afternoon on this deck design. A large platform is an inviting place to sit and read or spread out to catch some sun. A step down leads to the octagonal bay surrounded by floating benches—a perfect spot to set up a patio table and chairs.

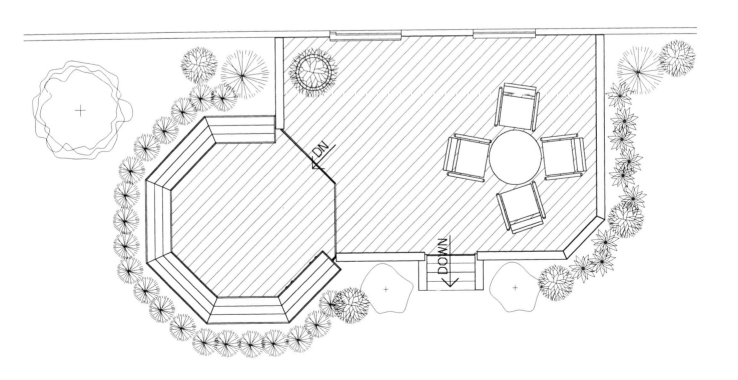

Photo courtesy of ©Decks USA, Inc.

This home, as shown in the photograph, may differ from the actual blueprints. For more detailed information, please check the floor plans carefully.

Design HPU050006

Square Footage: 288
Width: 26'-0" Depth: 18'-0"

This plan presents two sections separated by a flight of stairs. The upper level connects to the house and has diagonal flooring, while the octagonal lower platform sits to the left and has a built-in planter and stair access to the garden level.

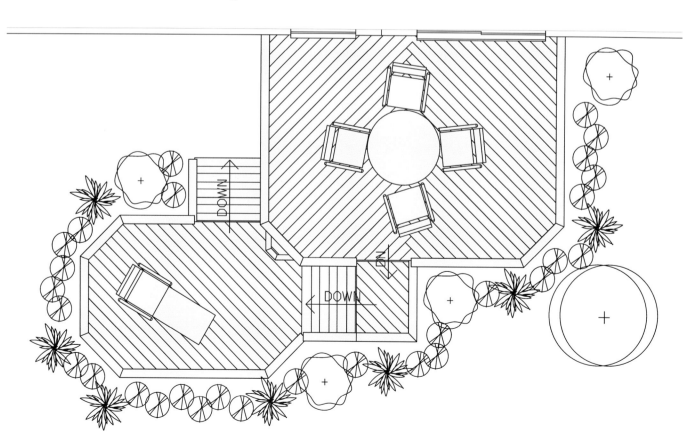

Photo courtesy of ©Decks USA, Inc.

This home, as shown in the photograph, may differ from the actual blueprints.
For more detailed information, please check the floor plans carefully.

Design HPU050007

Square Footage: 291
Width: 26'-0" Depth: 17'-0"

Planning on entertaining guests outside? Twin optional planters and freestanding benches are an elegant touch of symmetry. A step up introduces the dining bay, with plenty of room for casual meals. Two stairways make accessing the yard easy from both sides of the deck.

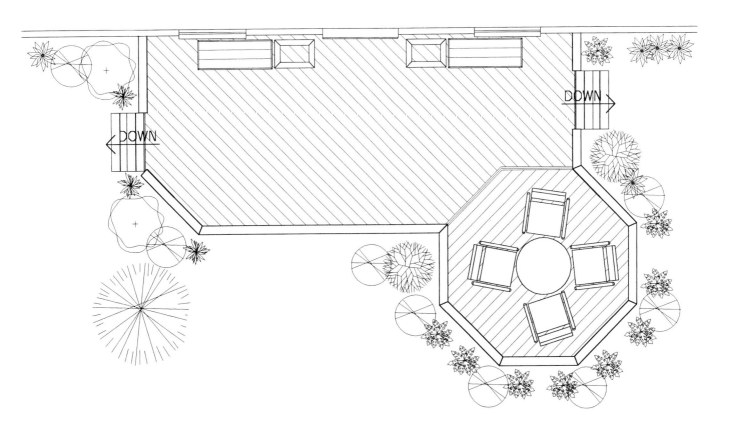

Design HPU050008
Square Footage: 292
Width: 26'-0" Depth: 17'-0"

*A*s an outdoor haven, this deck plan is sure to please. A long expanse welcomes a variety of outside activities such as grilling, summer parties, lounging in the sun and enjoying a fine meal during warm evenings. A dining bay will suit a more formal setting with plenty of room for a table.

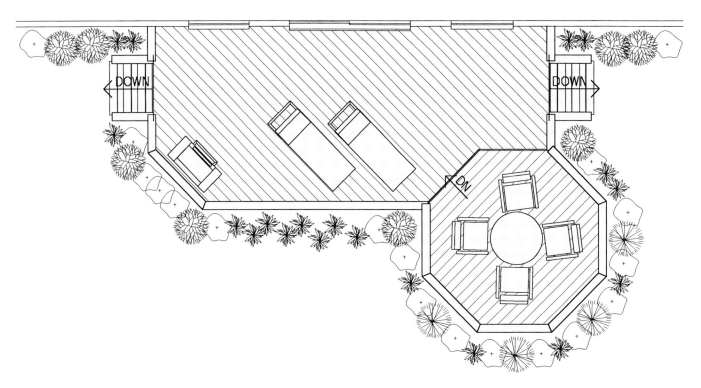

Photo courtesy of ©Decks USA, Inc.

This home, as shown in the photograph, may differ from the actual blueprints. For more detailed information, please check the floor plans carefully.

Design HPU050009
Square Footage: 307
Width: 20'-0" Depth: 19'-0"

*G*raduating spatial lines encourage a stylish simplicity in this deck design. A sitting bench flanked by large planters, three rail planters and a narrow stair are added accents that invite lush foliage, repose or casual entertaining.

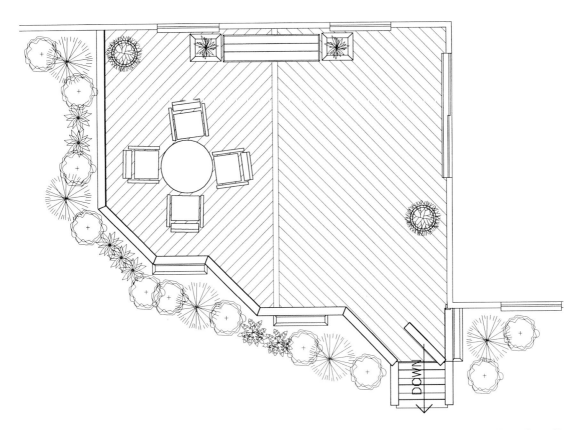

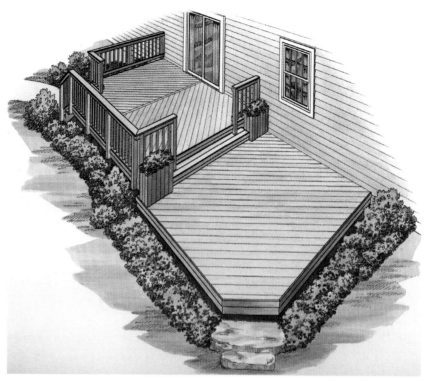

Design HPU050010

Square Footage: 313
Width: 27'-0" Depth: 12'-0"

Railing surrounds the upper level of this two-level deck while diagonal flooring adorns it. Two steps down, the lower level enjoys access to the yard from all sides.

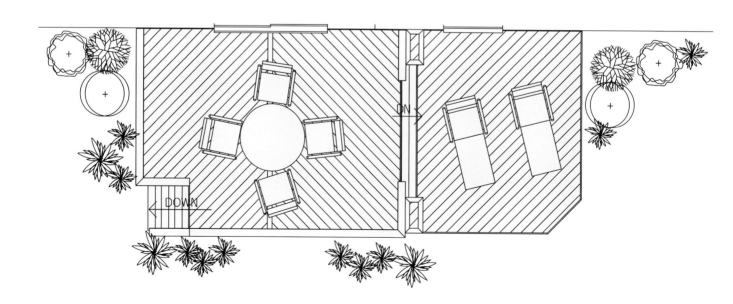

Photo courtesy of ©Decks USA, Inc.

This home, as shown in the photograph, may differ from the actual blueprints. For more detailed information, please check the floor plans carefully.

Design HPU050011
Square Footage: 362
Width: 28'-0" Depth: 14'-0"

*D*etails offer comfort for any occasion. Flared stairs welcome you to the twin-platform deck, which enjoys a whole side of floating benches, two bays, a set of box steps to the side and plenty of room for play.

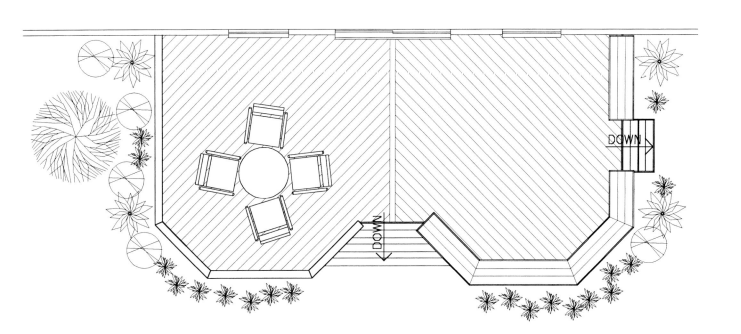

DOWN

DOWN

Photo courtesy of ©Decks USA, Inc.

This home, as shown in the photograph, may differ from the actual blueprints. For more detailed information, please check the floor plans carefully.

Design HPU050012

Square Footage: 370
Width: 27'-0" Depth: 15'-0"

*A*ngled stairs provide little intrusion into deck space. An optional built-in bench complements built-in flower boxes and would suit as a perfect dining area.

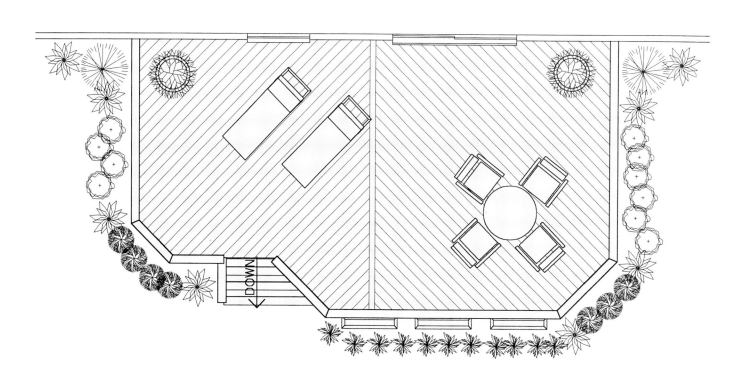

DOWN

This home, as shown in the photograph, may differ from the actual blueprints. For more detailed information, please check the floor plans carefully.

Design HPU050013

Square Footage: 374
Width: 47'-0" Depth: 17'-0"

*T*hree levels add dimension and character to this deck. Access the central deck via the stairs from the garden level or the upper level from the house. The middle and lower levels include freestanding benches.

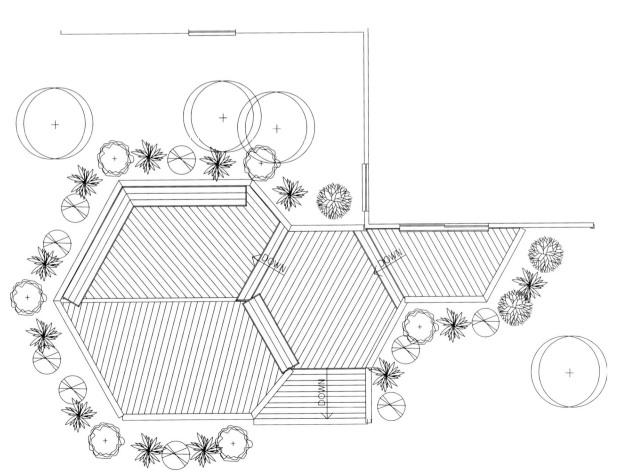

Design HPU050014

Square Footage: 383
Width: 24'-0" Depth: 26'-0"

A unique three-sided niche beautifies this L-shaped deck. Note the two stairways to the ground level and the extra length to the right side of the plan—providing plenty of entertainment space.

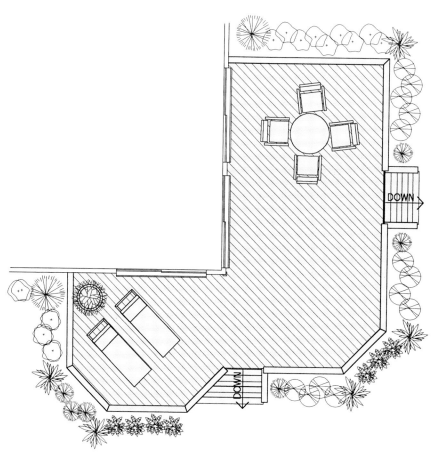

DOWN

DOWN

Design HPU050015
Square Footage: 420
Width: 30'-0" Depth: 15'-0"

*T*win platforms feature bumped-out bays—one for dining and one for a hot tub. Offering extra space for parties, grilling or relaxation, this design is made for those who revel in the sun.

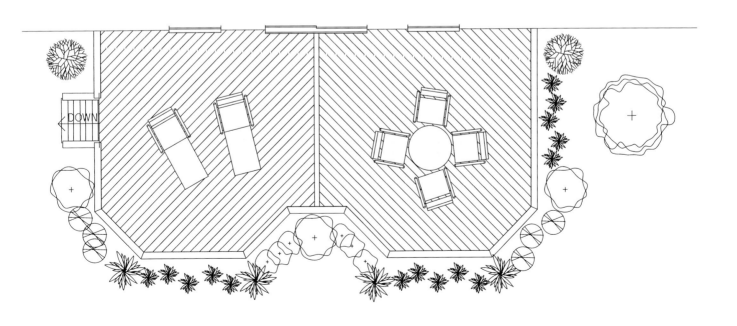

DOWN

Design HPU050016

Square Footage: 439
Width: 33'-0" Depth: 16'-0"

This deck easily suits a house built on a sloping lot. Rails surround the entire deck area, with two benches to the left. The stairs lead to the garden level from the right lower level. The plan can include optional rail planters and additional freestanding benches.

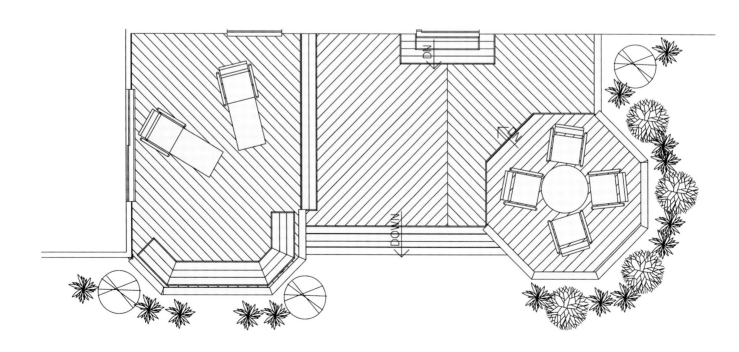

Photo courtesy of ©Decks USA, Inc.

This home, as shown in the photograph, may differ from the actual blueprints. For more detailed information, please check the floor plans carefully.

Design HPU050017
Square Footage: 459
Width: 37'-0" Depth: 20'-0"

*D*esigned to wrap around the left of the home's rear elevation, this deck provides plenty of space for outdoor entertainment. Rails surround the entire deck, while the lower section—just one step down—features box steps to the garden level.

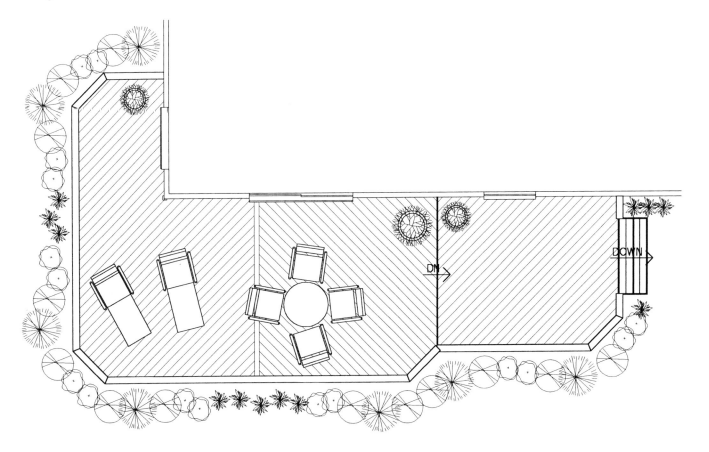

Photo courtesy of ©Decks USA, Inc.

This home, as shown in the photograph, may differ from the actual blueprints. For more detailed information, please check the floor plans carefully.

Design HPU050018
Square Footage: 476
Width: 32'-0" Depth: 24'-0"

*T*wo half-octagonal alcoves shape the main section of this deck, while a set of stairs leads to the ground level between them. Down one step, a second platform wraps around the house and offers a second set of stairs.

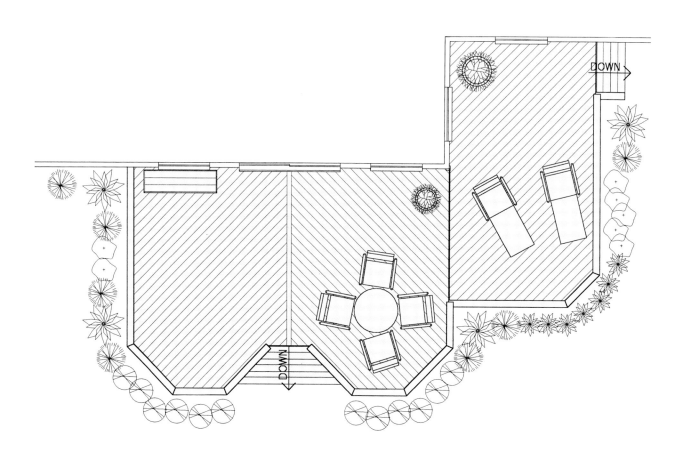

This home, as shown in the photograph, may differ from the actual blueprints. For more detailed information, please check the floor plans carefully.

Design HPU050019

Square Footage: 499
Width: 35'-0" Depth: 15'-0"

*T*his enchanting deck will enhance any home. Angled stairs lead from the left, via a gate, while three-sided niches are interposed into the body of the plan. A step and rails separate the two sections of the design. Optional rail planters and freestanding benches will add to the charm.

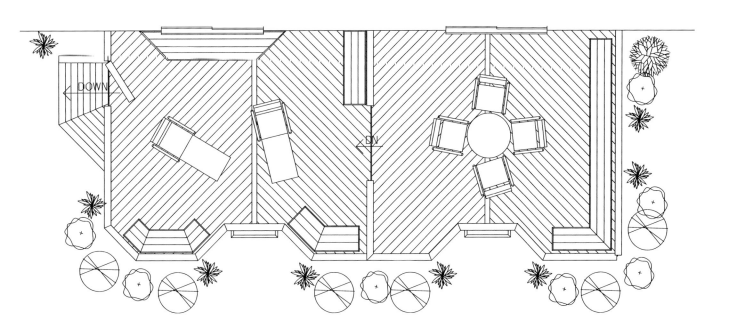

Design HPU050020

Square Footage: 593
Width: 40'-0" Depth: 22'-0"

This deck easily suits a house built on a sloping lot. Rails surround the entire deck area, with two benches to the left. The stairs lead to the garden level from the right lower level. The plan can include optional rail planters and additional freestanding benches.

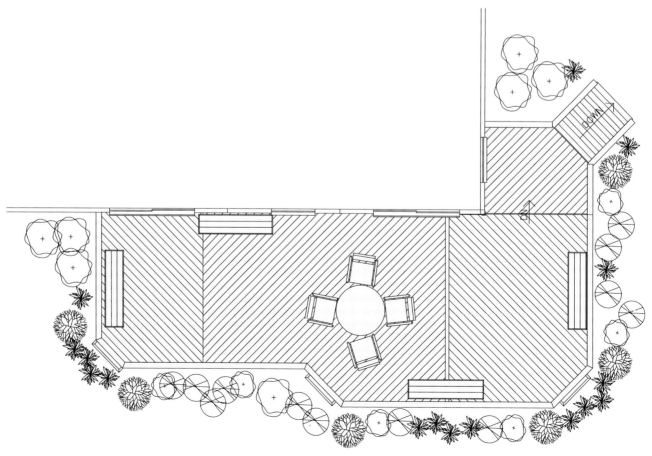

Design HPU050021
Square Footage: 90
Width: 10'-0" Depth: 9'-0"

A simple shape goes a long way for smaller yards. This basic square offers a perfect area for outside dining and grilling, with access to the rest of the yard from the side stairway.

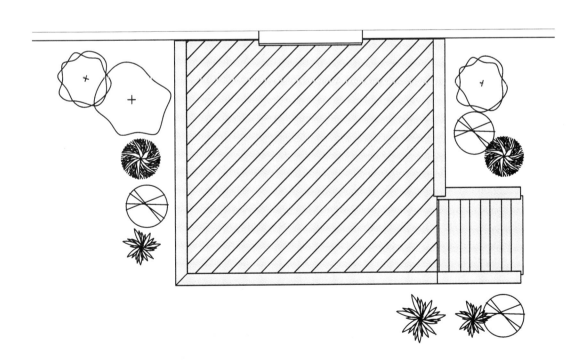

Design HPU050022
Square Footage: 136
Width: 18'-0" Depth: 10'-0"

*I*nterested in angles? Try this design. Flared stairs lead to a spacious bay, perfect for a garden table or spa. With plenty of space leftover for extra seating or a grill, this deck is an eye-pleaser.

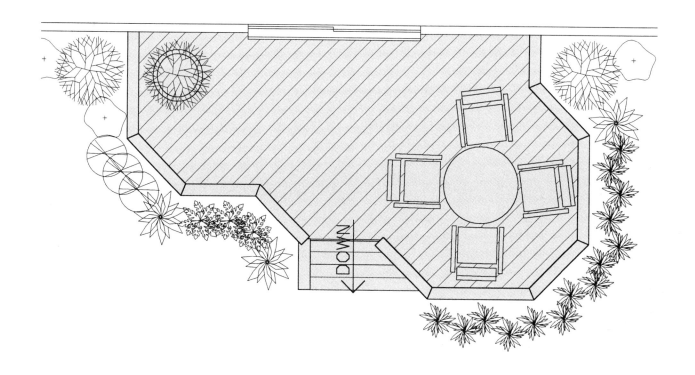

DOWN

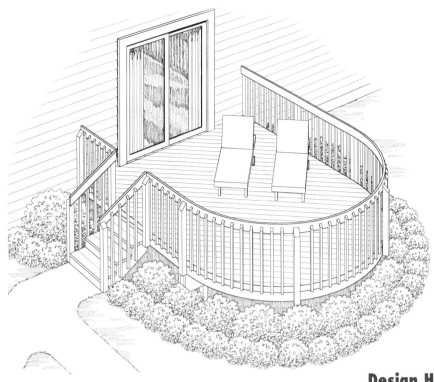

Design HPU050023
Square Footage: 176
Width: 12'-0" Depth: 16'-0"

*A*s long as you have twelve feet of space, this deck will fit your site. Twelve feet by sixteen feet and circular shaped, this deck will add beautiful outdoor days to your year. Note the stairs from the left side of the deck to the ground level.

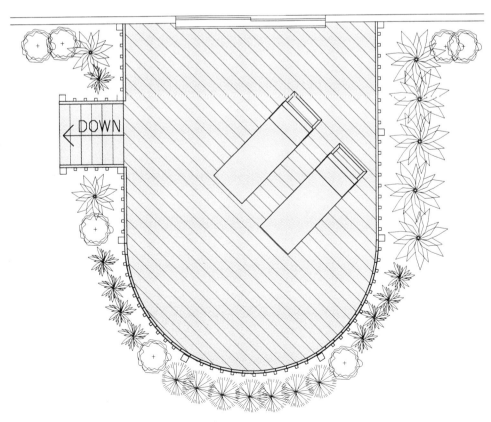

DOWN

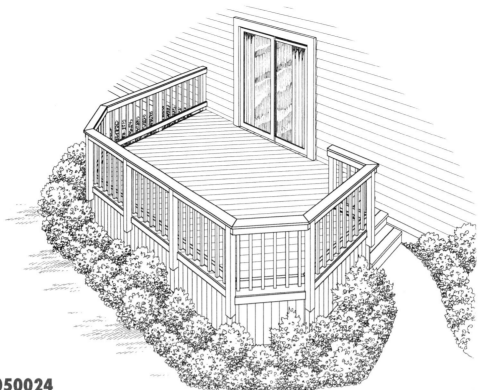

Design HPU050024
Square Footage: 147
Width: 16'-0" Depth: 10'-0"

Straighter lines give this plan uncomplicated appeal without sacrificing space. The dining bay sits just inside the stairway—a few steps to the yard beyond.

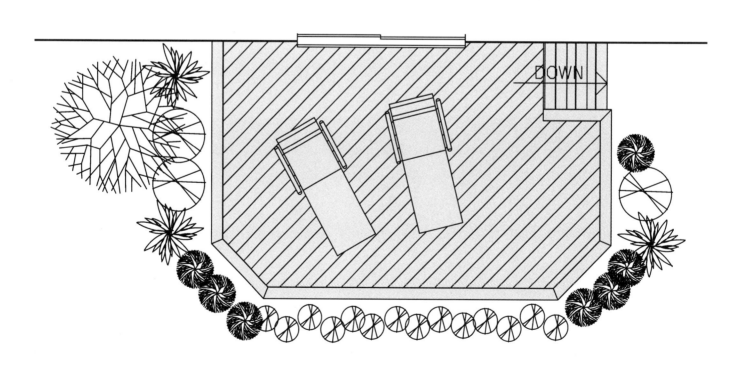

DOWN

Design HPU050025
Square Footage: 147
Width: 13'-0" Depth: 12'-0"

*E*asy to attach to the front, side or rear of the house, this deck will add outdoor livability anywhere. The plan includes stairs from the left side of the deck to ground level and a charming safety rail around the half-octagonal contour of the deck.

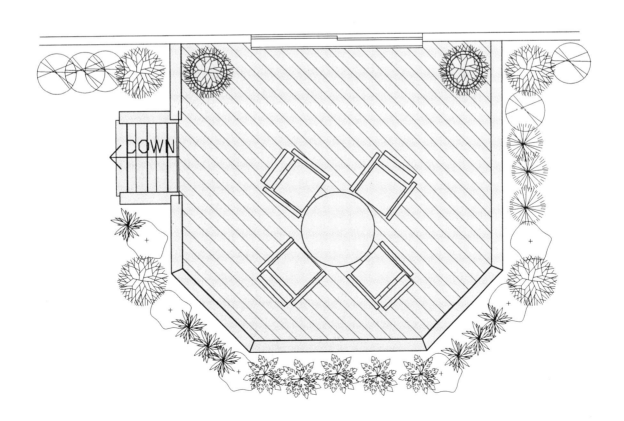

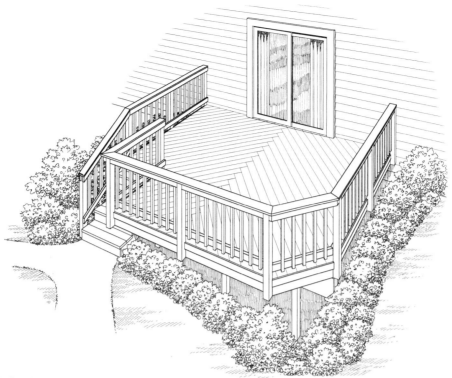

Design HPU050026

Square Footage: 166
Width: 15'-0" Depth: 12'-0"

This simple design will complement a narrow footprint or provide just the right amount of extra living space in tight spots. Set up a grill and dining furniture for a casual get-together out of doors.

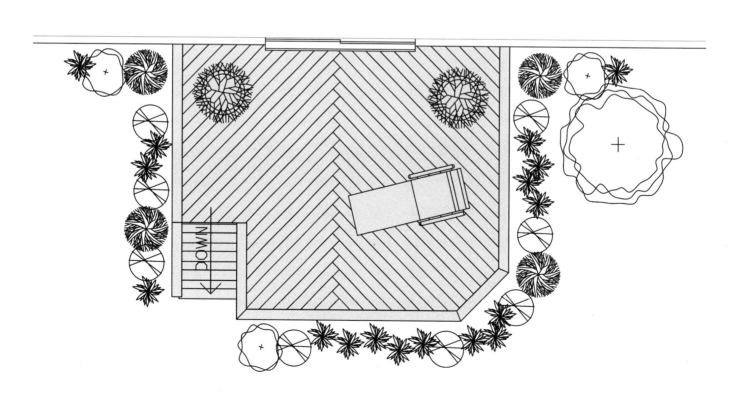

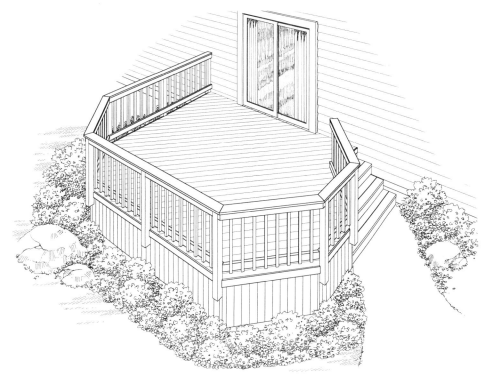

Design HPU050027

Square Footage: 170
Width: 16'-0" Depth: 12'-0"

*T*his open, gazebo-like design is a spectacular addition for outdoor living space. With a dining bay near the angled stairs and away from the home entrance, meals can be comfortable without being crowded.

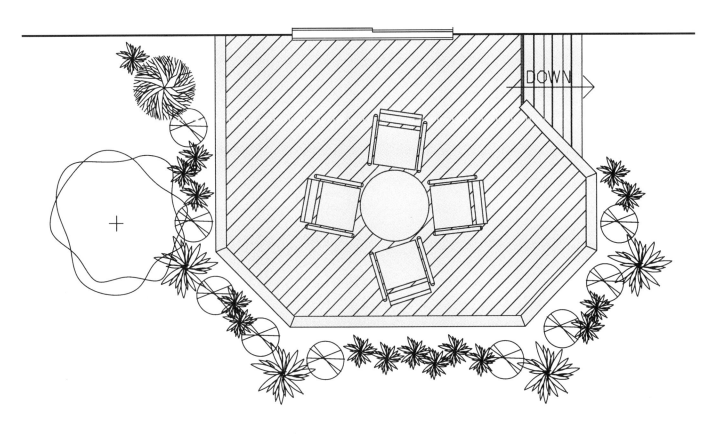

DOWN

Design HPU050028

Square Footage: 211
Width: 21'-3" Depth: 14'-3"

*A*ngled stairs open to a bay that's perfect for a spa or extra dining space. The roomy platform can handle the energy of entertaining or the leisure of repose.

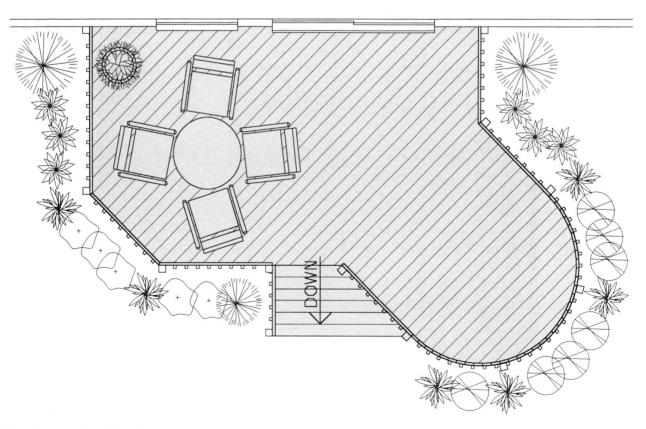

DOWN

Design HPU050029
Square Footage: 202
Width: 18'-0" Depth: 13'-0"

*T*he simplicity of this design will fit any style home and it offers a perfect place to read the morning paper or have that cup of coffee. A deep stair provides interaction with the yard beyond.

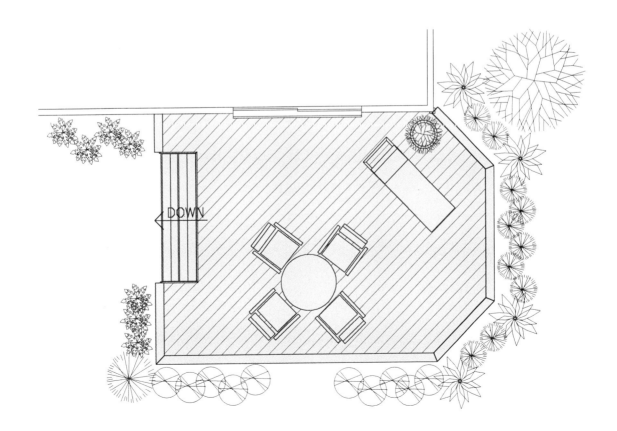

DOWN

Design HPU050030

Square Footage: 203
Width: 19'-0" Depth: 14'-0"

A small area with plenty of living can be found on this deck. A large bay is useful for dining or a great spot for the spa. A simple box step to the side keeps the platform from being too open and regulates foot traffic.

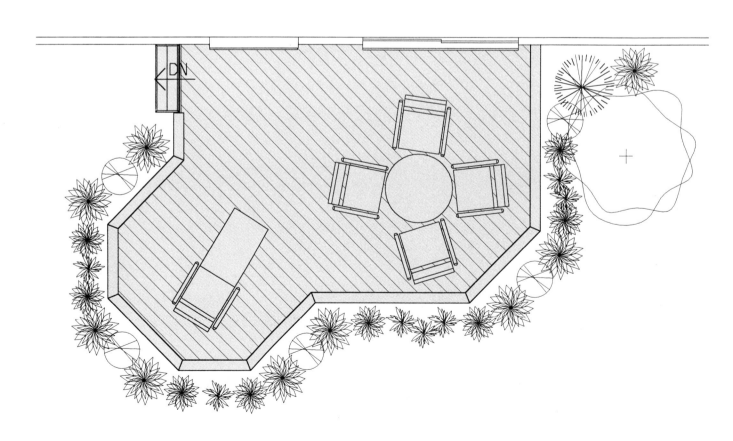

Design HPU050031
Square Footage: 204
Width: 27'-0" Depth: 9'-0"

*T*his extra-long deck offers two stairs accessing the yard, complete railing and a large bumped-out bay. If space is a concern and outdoor dining, gardening or taking advantage of views are important, this design will fit the bill.

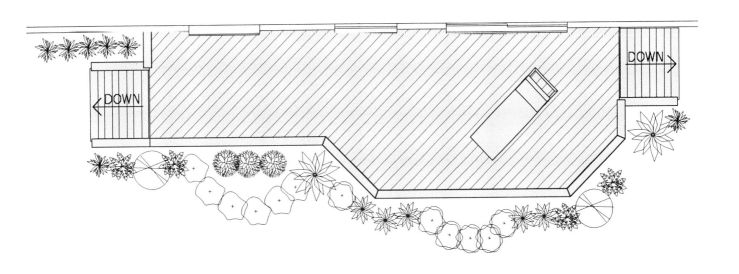

Design HPU050032

Square Footage: 222
Width: 22'-0" Depth: 17'-0"

Two decks in one! A small platform is great for a grill or herb garden and is only steps away from the stairs, which access the yard. A larger area is just around the corner and would do well to expand the dining area to the comfortable outdoors.

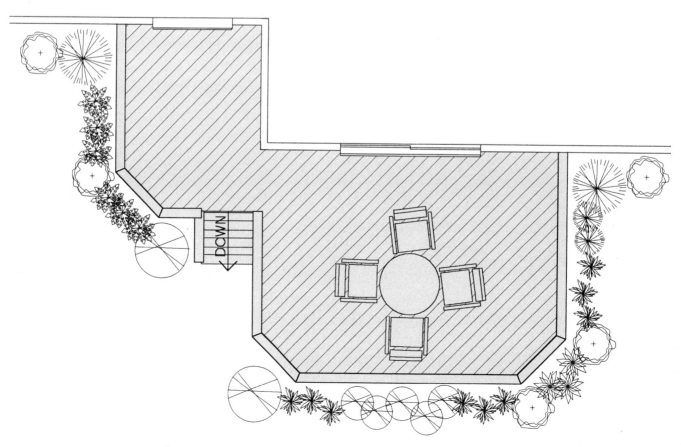

DOWN

Design HPU050033

Square Footage: 223
Width: 17'-0" Depth: 15'-0"

*T*win bays offer both dining and spa areas for complete outdoor living. Relax in the spa bay, which features a half-octagonal floating bench for dipping feet or sunning. Open deck space is ideal for other recreational pursuits.

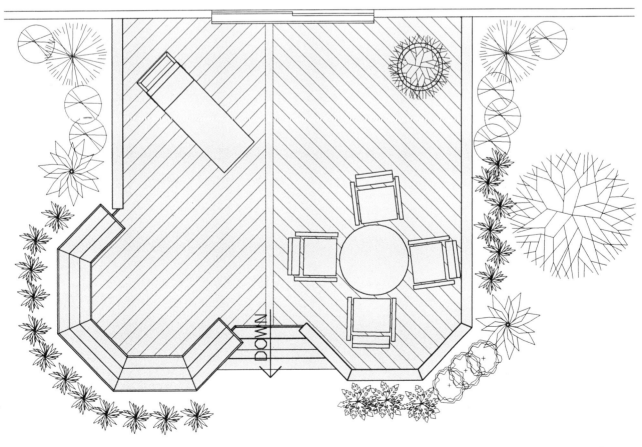

Design HPU050034
Square Footage: 230
Width: 20'-0" Depth: 12'-0"

*W*rapping around one side of this plan is a built-in bench flanked by planters with a short stair nearby. From this point, space radiates to fit furniture, plants and a grilling station or just to enjoy open space. An angled stair leads to the yard.

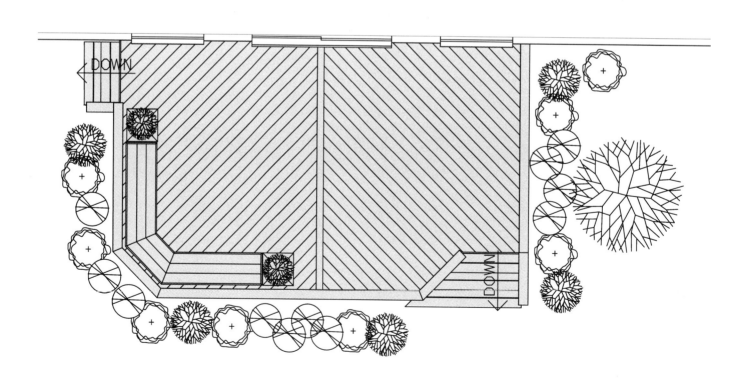

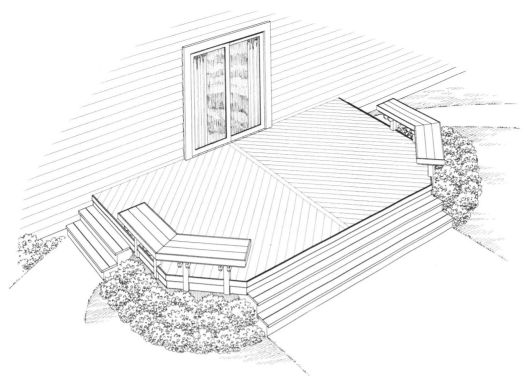

Design HPU050035
Square Footage: 231
Width: 20'-0" Depth: 12'-0"

*F*loating benches and three stairways make this deck design an open entry to the yard beyond. The wide platform is a great place to stretch out and relax with a cool meal or a small gathering of friends for a barbecue on a sunny afternoon.

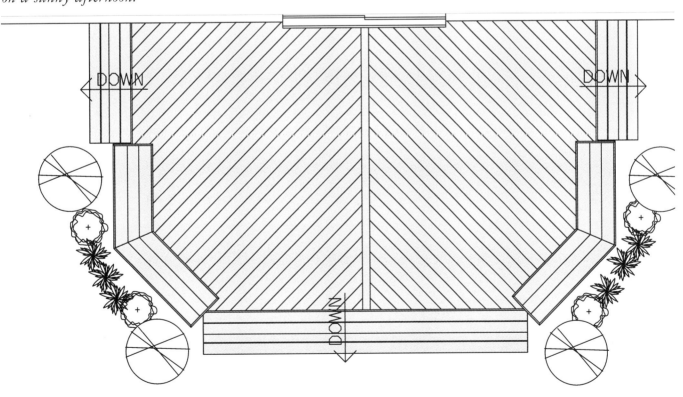

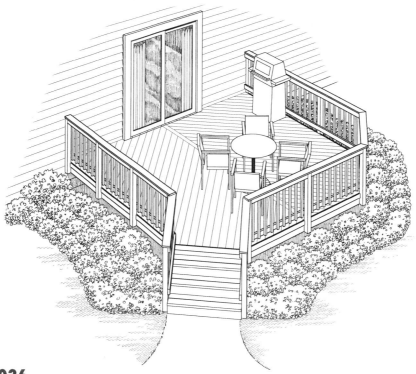

Design HPU050036

Square Footage: 231
Width: 16'-0" Depth: 15'-0"

*S*tairs lead from the left corner of this deck, echoing the decorative angled flooring. With 16' x 15' dimensions, this area will add outdoor livability to your home.

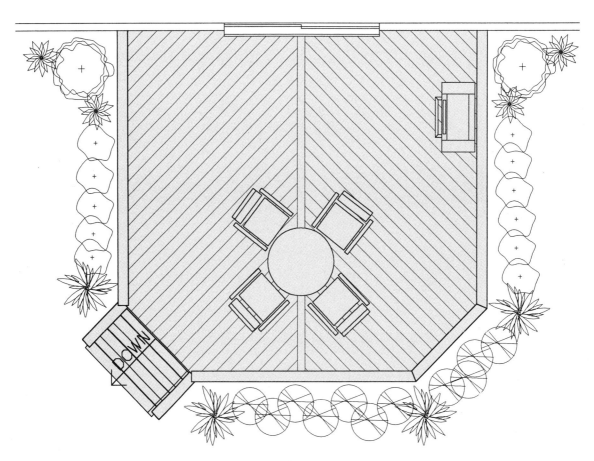

Design HPU050037

Square Footage: 231
Width: 16'-0" Depth: 15'-0"

*W*ith room for a barbecue grill and lounge chairs, this 16' x 15' foot deck will make your summer extra special. A set of stairs connects the ground level to the deck level on the left side. Note the decorative angle of the flooring.

DOWN

Design HPU050038

Square Footage: 231
Width: 16'-0" Depth: 15'-0"

*A*dd a room-size deck to your livable space with this half-octagon plan. Stairs to the left fit snugly against the house, and diagonal flooring adds dimension to this plan.

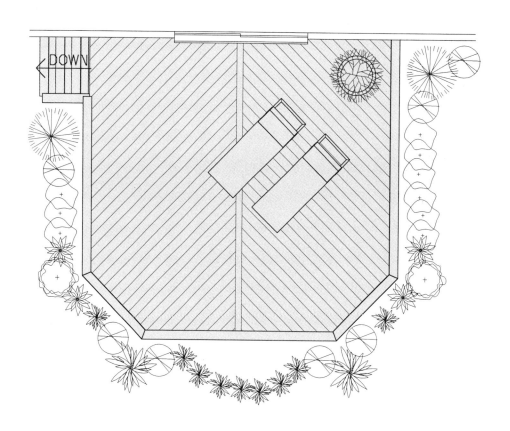

DOWN

Design HPU050039
Square Footage: 231
Width: 16'-0" Depth: 16'-0"

A V-shape in the flooring enhances the octagon contour of this deck. Stairs lead from the front to the garden level.

Design HPU050040

Square Footage: 232
Width: 16'-0" Depth: 10'-0"

This unique design offers maximum use of a narrow space. Triangular in shape with a stairway, this deck features enough room for cookouts and leisure furniture and is just right for a garden view.

DOWN

Design HPU050041
Square Footage: 236
Width: 15'-0" Depth: 16'-0"

*T*his corner deck will fit nicely into a limited space. A curved railing allows you to enjoy the view or add a table and a few chairs for casual meals.

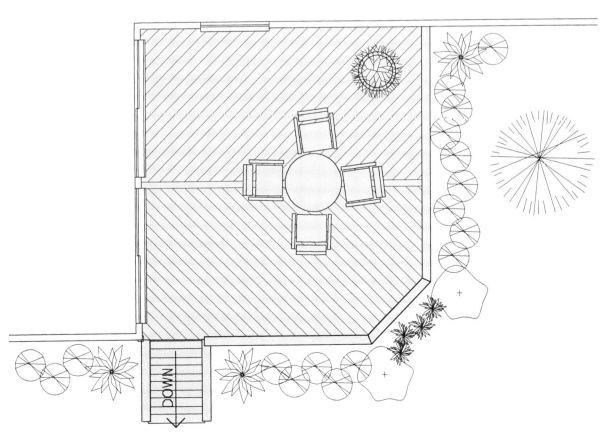

DOWN

Design HPU050042
Square Footage: 238
Width: 27'-0" Depth: 10'-0"

*T*hree sections can be used for dining, lounge furniture, a grill, herb garden, telescope or spa on this long deck. Outdoor entertaining will be easy with so much space. Long lines will accentuate a spectacular view.

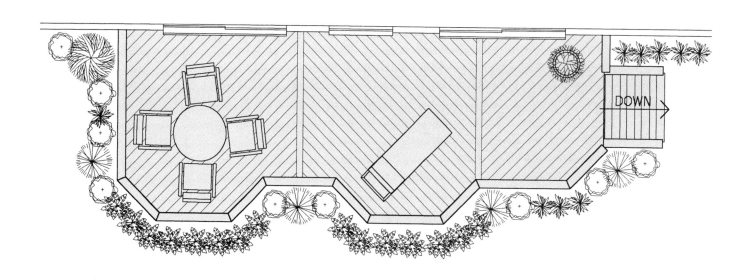

DOWN →

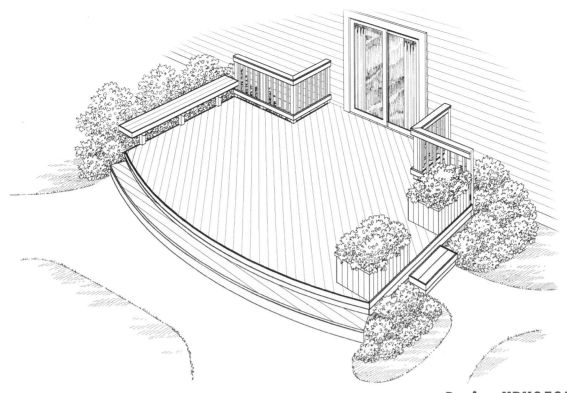

Design HPU050043

Square Footage: 265
Width: 20'-0" Depth: 16'-0"

*S*traight lines open up this deck to enjoy a lovely landscape. A floating bench offers seating, while curved steps run the length of the deck. Twin planters and another step keep the pattern open with a touch of privacy.

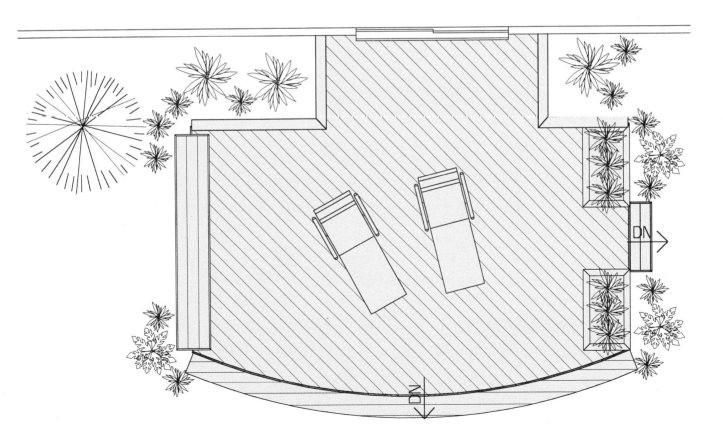

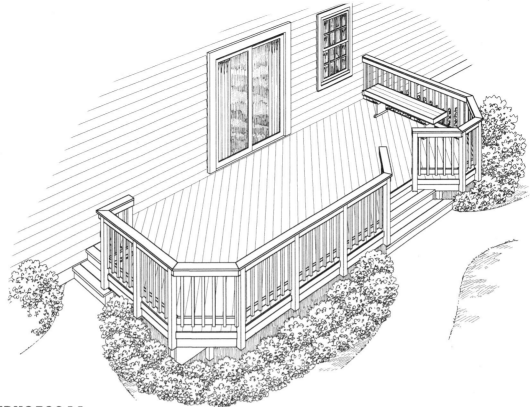

Design HPU050044

Square Footage: 244
Width: 24'-0" Depth: 11'-0"

*S*ide stairs and angled entrance stairs provide convenient access to the yard. A small bay gives the option of a freestanding bench for extra, casual seating while a more spacious bay is ideal for alfresco dining for a few or several guests.

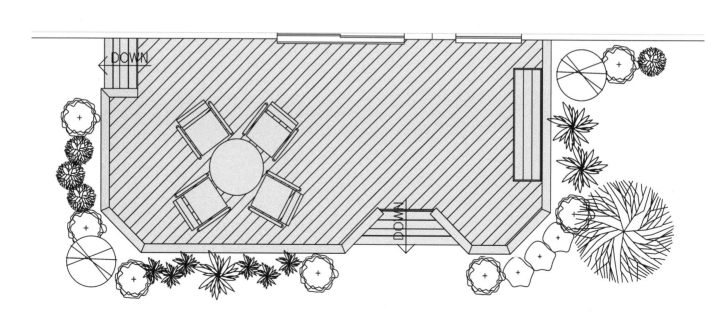

Design HPU050045
Square Footage: 249
Width: 24'-0" Depth: 14'-0"

*A*great design to step out to on sunny days and warm nights. A raised bay could be used as a dining area or a spa retreat, while the rest of the deck serves as entertaining space or a nice spot for a potted garden.

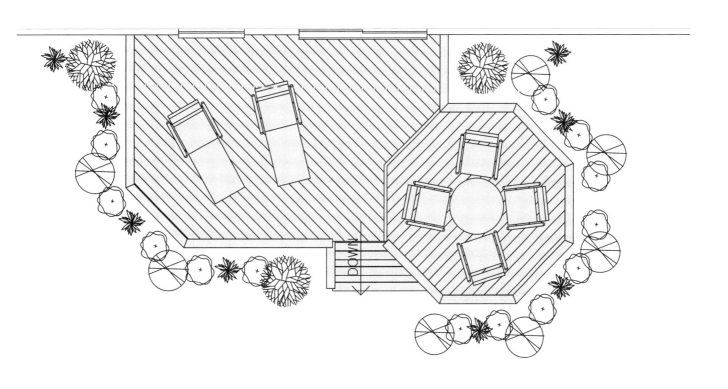

Design HPU050046

Square Footage: 254
Width: 20'-0" Depth: 14'-0"

*S*eating is the focus of this plan. With floating benches outlining the deck area, entertaining guests and capturing great views from three sides is as simple as walking out onto this deck.

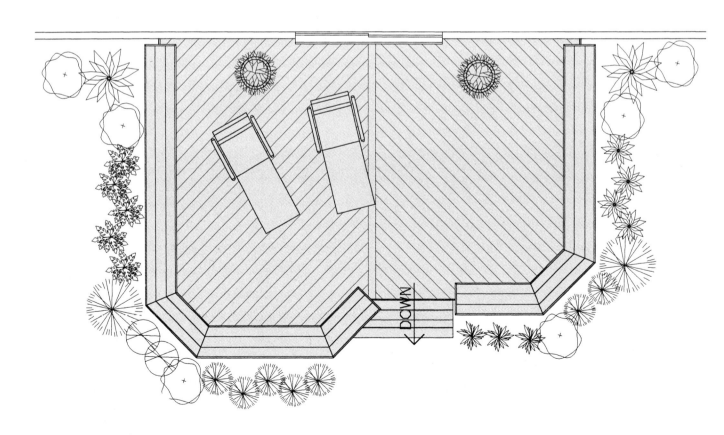

DOWN

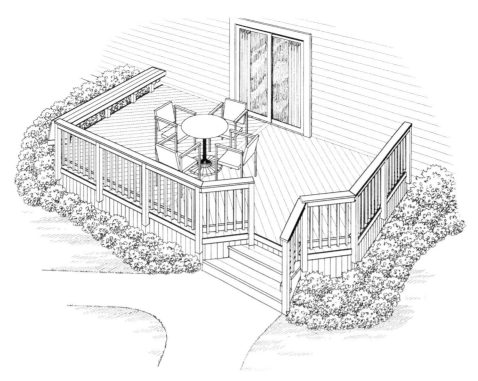

Design HPU050047
Square Footage: 257
Width: 21'-0" Depth: 13'-0"

*M*ake excellent use of extra outdoor space with this deck design! A floating bench offers a whole side of built-in seating, which opens up the rest of the deck for comfortable leisure furnishings, a grilling station, potted garden or just breathing room.

Design HPU050048
Square Footage: 258
Width: 22'-0" Depth: 13'-0"

*A*n elegant presentation makes all the difference with this design. A great layout for multi-use space, the stairs are located to the side so traffic flow won't detract from casual get-togethers or larger events. Front scallops create two half-bays and a large central bay.

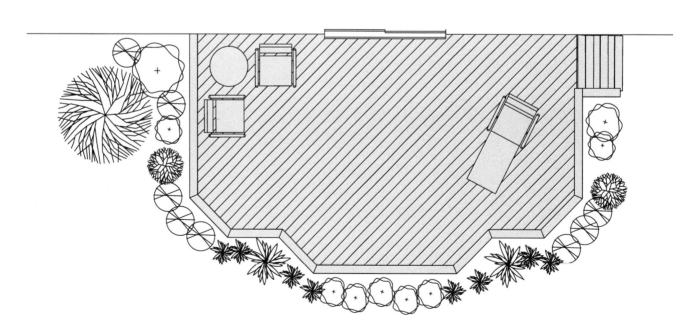

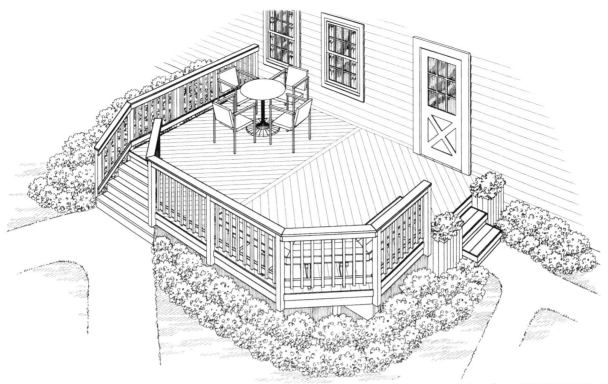

Design HPU050049

Square Footage: 267
Width: 19'-0" Depth: 15'-0"

A simple platform with many amenities will conspire to improve the view without wasting space. An angled stair leads to a large bay, just right for dining, with built-in bench seating to accommodate guests. Another stair is positioned between attractive planters near the bay.

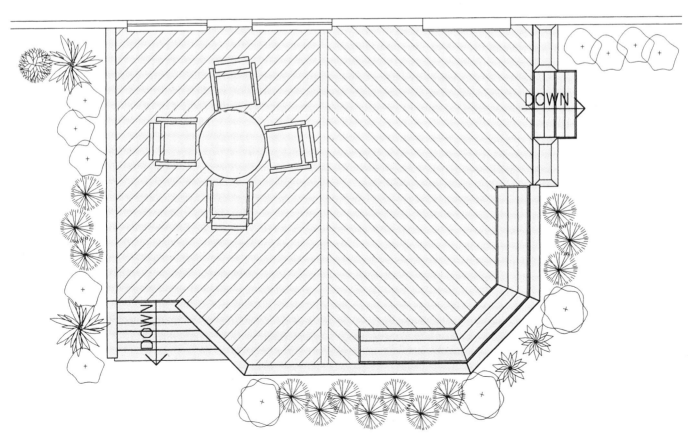

Design HPU050050

Square Footage: 269
Width: 22'-0" Depth: 15'-0"

Looking for a deck that makes great use of an odd shape? This design features an angled stairway to the yard, a bay for dining or a spa and a squared, jutting bay that's perfect as an overlook or for a telescope.

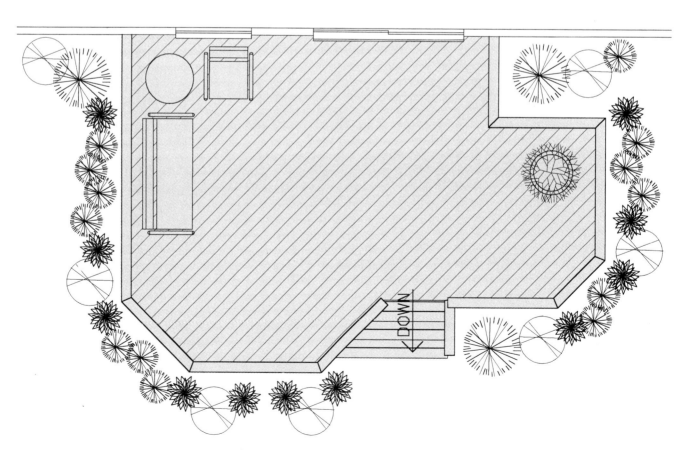

Design HPU050051
Square Footage: 270
Width: 25'-0" Depth: 15'-0"

*E*xtra amenities include a step-up octagonal bay surrounded by floating bench seating and a smaller bay near angled stairs to the yard. The octagonal bay is an idyllic spot for a spa, with views on all sides. The smaller area may be used as dining space or for extra seating.

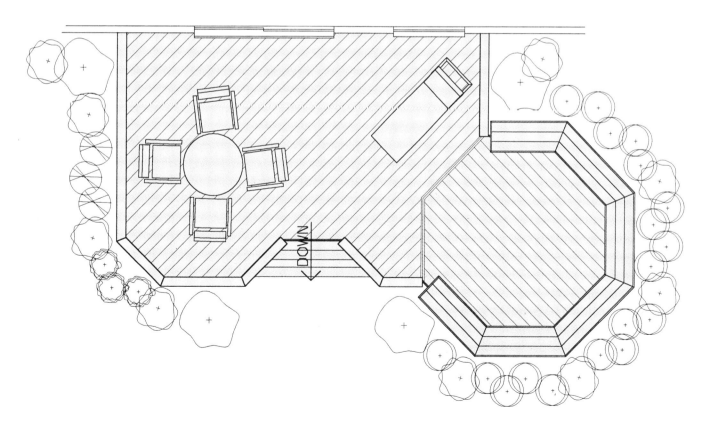

DOWN

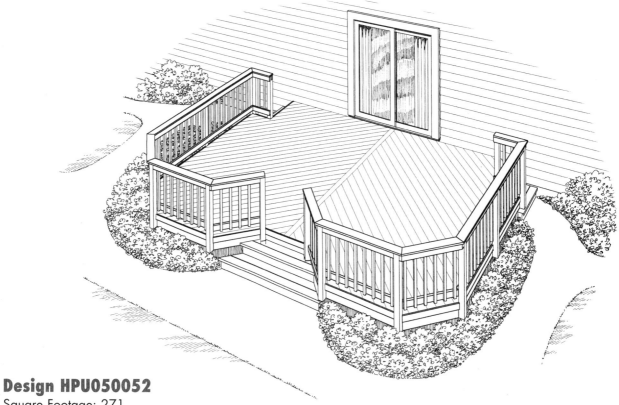

Design HPU050052

Square Footage: 271
Width: 20'-0" Depth: 15'-0"

Symmetry never looked so good! Equal spacing, twin bays, side stairways and centered stairs leading to the yard will accommodate all your leisurely pursuits. Dining, dips in the spa, a grand entrance to the garden or a vantage-point for a priceless vista make this deck a smart choice.

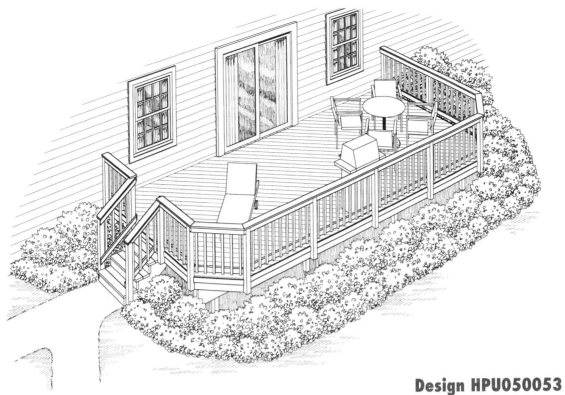

Design HPU050053
Square Footage: 284
Width: 24'-0" Depth: 12'-0"

*T*his basic deck will span a full twenty-four feet of the house. The rounded edges are echoed with the safety railing, and a set of stairs leads from the left down to the garden level.

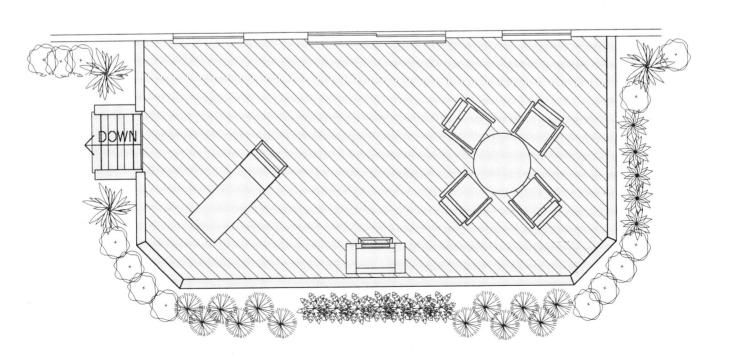

DOWN

Design HPU050054

Square Footage: 285
Width: 24'-0" Depth: 13'-0"

*W*alk out onto this deck and take in the view. A wide bay provides plenty of room for dining and leisure furniture. Set up the grill in the corner or to the side of the stairs for an outdoor repast, while enjoying the weather.

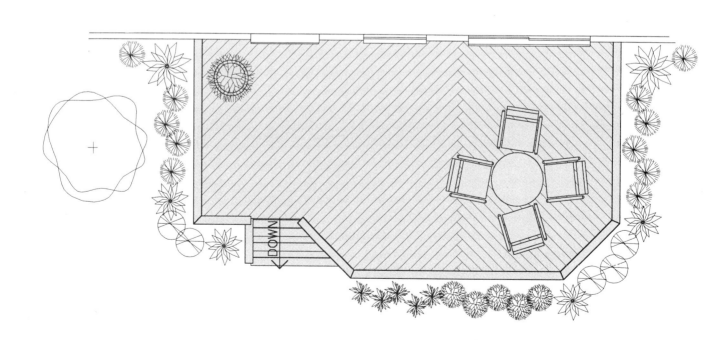

DOWN

Design HPU050055
Square Footage: 286
Width: 24'-0" Depth: 12'-0"

*T*his straightforward design is made for a space that can accommodate long lines. With stairs at the front left and plenty of space, this deck is open for any number of pursuits. Add a dining table, grill and plants for a cool place to hang out in the evening.

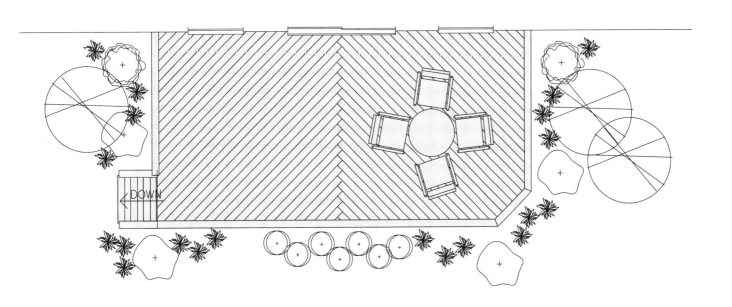

DOWN

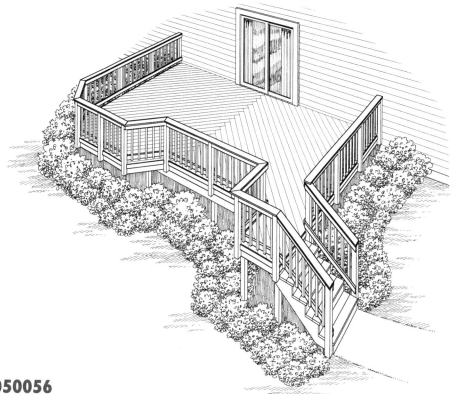

Design HPU050056

Square Footage: 289
Width: 22'-0" Depth: 15'-0"

*T*his deck's long footprint features separate space for a dining area and a relaxing spa retreat. The stairway is completely unobtrusive with a bumped-out platform to direct traffic.

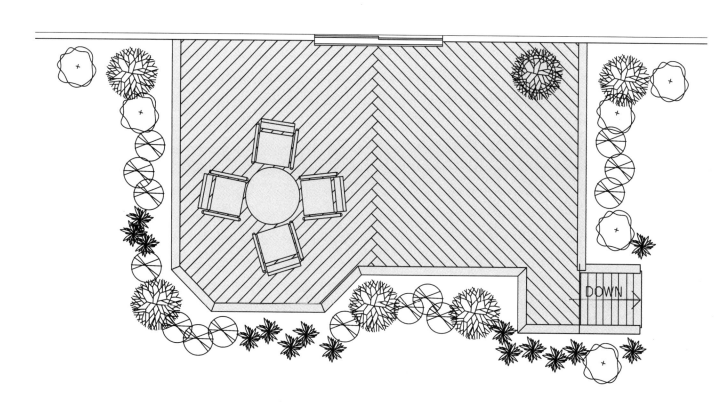

DOWN

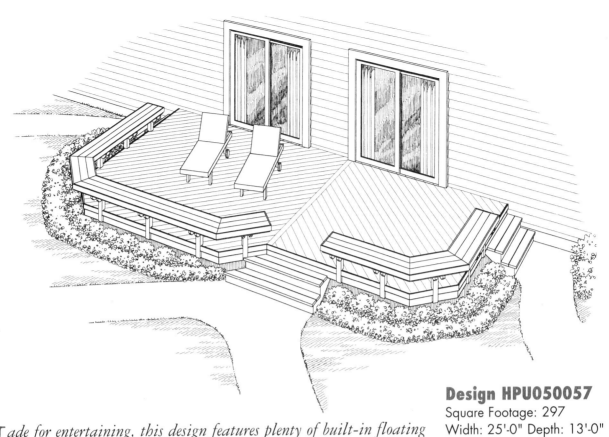

Design HPU050057
Square Footage: 297
Width: 25'-0" Depth: 13'-0"

*M*ade for entertaining, this design features plenty of built-in floating benches. Three stairways provide access to the yard at different points and make a crowd more manageable. A larger portion is great for larger activities, while a smaller area is ideal for dining.

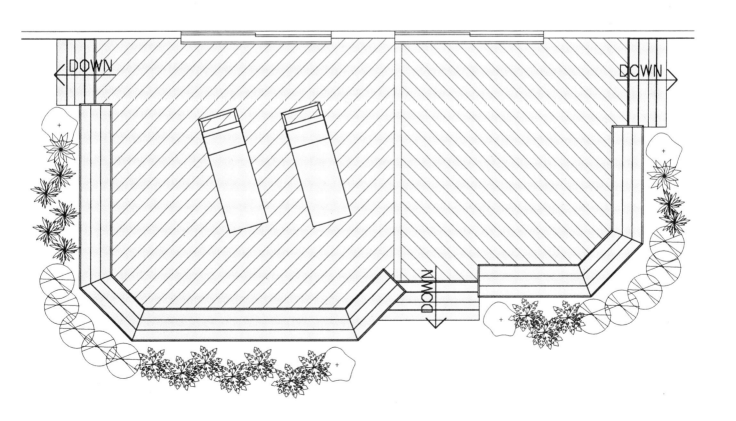

DOWN

DOWN

DOWN

Design HPU050058
Square Footage: 299
Width: 22'-0" Depth: 15'-6"

This plan is a snug fit for an open corner. Offering a living extension to the rear or side yard, this plan provides great interaction with the outdoors.

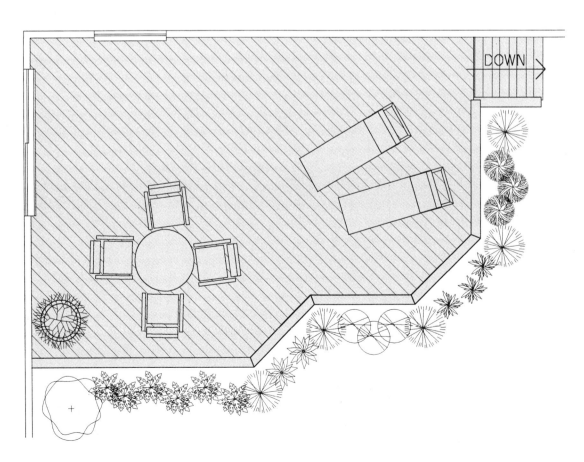

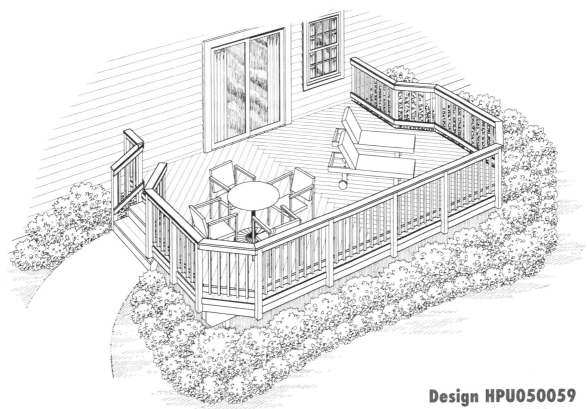

Design HPU050059
Square Footage: 302
Width: 22'-0" Depth: 15'-0"

*T*his design is fit for extended outdoor living, with room for alfresco dining, a lush potted garden, extra seating or just stargazing. Stairs lead to the yard beyond, while a full railing offers security.

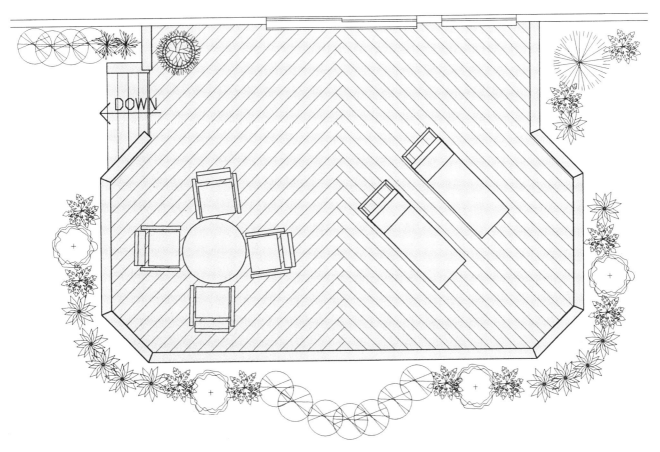

DOWN

Design HPU050060

Square Footage: 306
Width: 24'-0" Depth: 14'-0"

*A*n oversized area awaits moderate gatherings or recreational activities and another, smaller platform is just right for intimate dinners or casual events and makes this an ideal complement to any yard. The side railing encloses the deck without minimizing wonderful views.

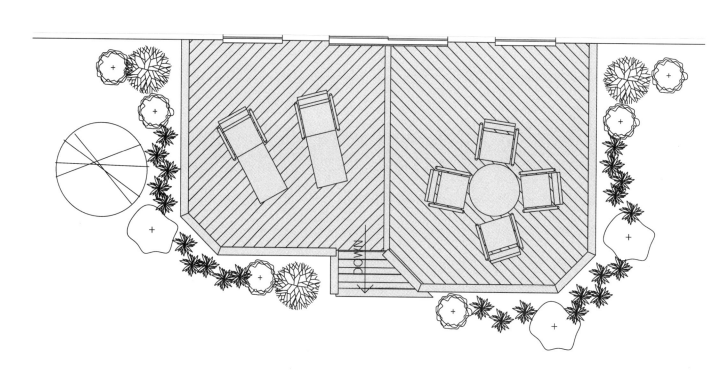

Design HPU050061

Square Footage: 312
Width: 27'-0" Depth: 12'-0"

*D*esigned to extend living space to the outdoors, this plan is perfect for alfresco dining. Angled stairs open to a subtle dining bay on the right and a larger multi-use area to the left. Add furniture and a grilling station for casual entertaining.

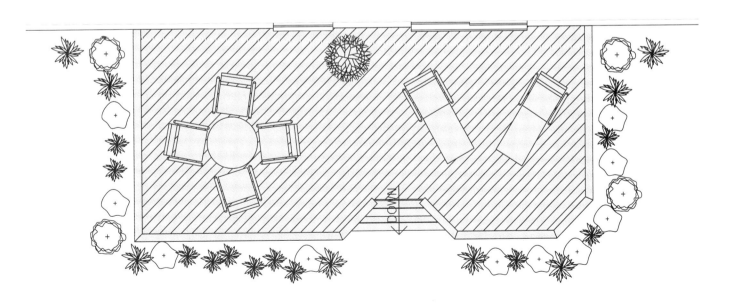

Design HPU050062

Square Footage: 352
Width: 30'-0" Depth: 17'-0"

Designed to fit around a home with multiple doorways, this deck enjoys a dining bay and two stairways to the yard. The remainder of the platform is ideal for entertaining activities and adding interest to the house and yard.

Design HPU050063

Square Footage: 354
Width: 26'-0" Depth: 15'-0"

*T*his great design accentuates a lovely landscape or view with varying lines. There is plenty of room for a garden table and lounging area, with an optional free-standing bench to accommodate extra guests or individual moments of peace and quiet.

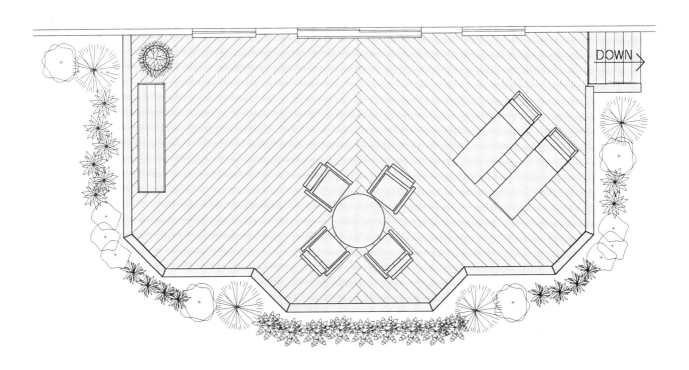

Design HPU050064

Square Footage: 369
Width: 26'-0" Depth: 15'-0"

This rectangular deck provides center stairs to the yard beyond, an optional bench seat and two bays with open railing. Enjoy a starlit dinner or a dip in the hot tub while relaxing outdoors.

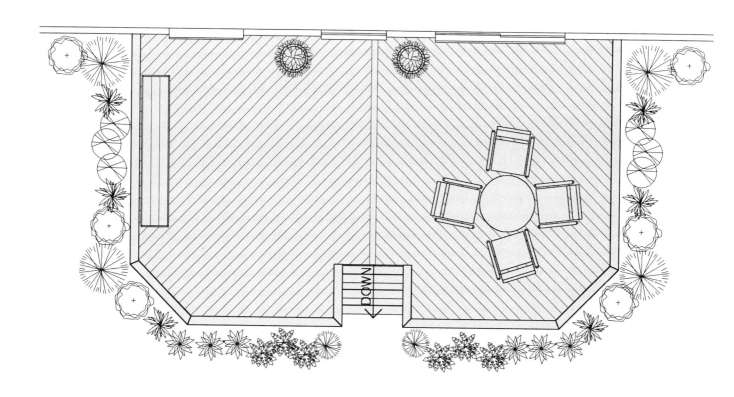

Design HPU050065
Square Footage: 393
Width: 32'-0" Depth: 15'-0"

*T*he gradual tapering effect of this deck will complement any size yard. A wide stair opens to the deepest part of the deck. Planters and a freestanding bench offer interest and seating for the more narrow areas.

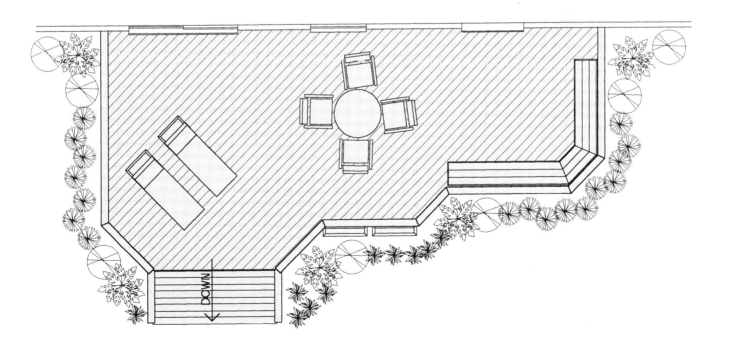

DOWN

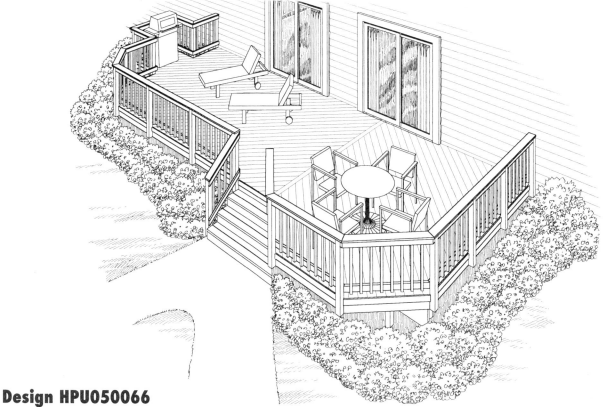

Design HPU050066
Square Footage: 394
Width: 38'-0" Depth: 15'-0"

*W*ide-open spaces right outside the door! With a built-in grill area, dining bay and plenty of space in between, this design takes alfresco meals to a new level. Flared stairs add a touch of class and access the grounds beyond in a few steps.

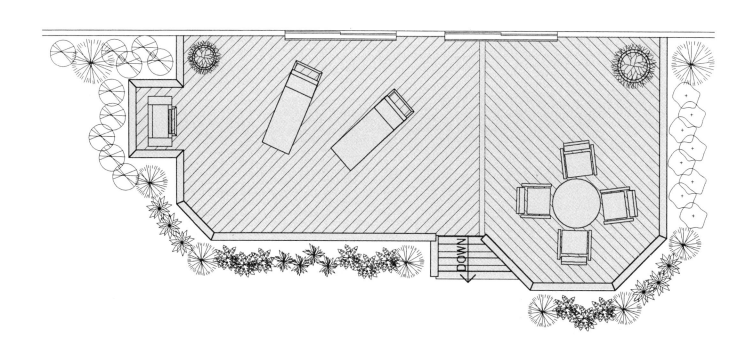

DOWN

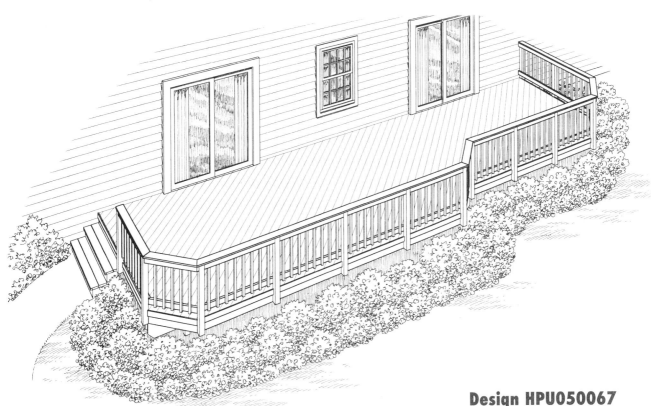

Design HPU050067
Square Footage: 398
Width: 36'-0" Depth: 12'-0"

*L*ong, simple lines offer multi-use space with this plan. A wide area can be used for dining, a spa, or just relaxing in a comfortable chair. Stairs provide access to the yard and an unobstructed line to the narrower deck area.

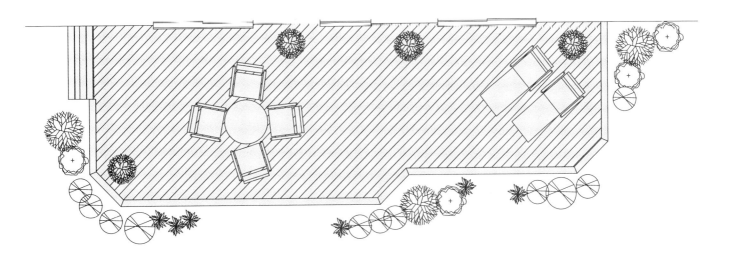

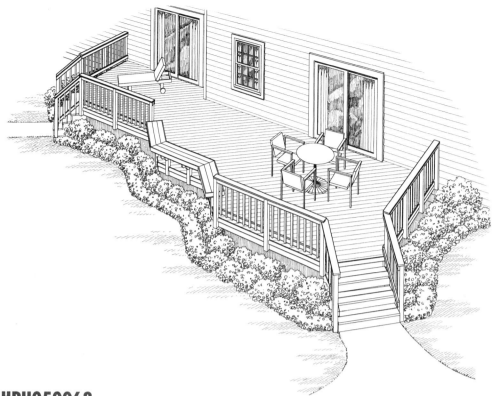

Design HPU050068

Square Footage: 400
Width: 36'-0" Depth: 16'-0"

A ngles abound to take advantage of a great view or a hard-to-fit lot.
A floating bench offers built-in seating. This deck enjoys plenty of
room for tables, a barbecue, an outside kitchen, potted garden or just a place
to enjoy the panorama.

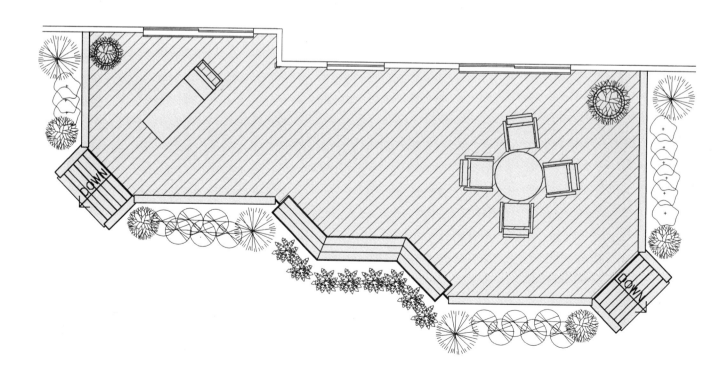

Design HPU050069
Square Footage: 416
Width: 35'-0" Depth: 14'-0"

*T*his deck offers quite a bit of outdoor space. Built-in seating can be found in a bay and a storage bench sits along the wall. Stairs provide access to the yard and streamline traffic flow.

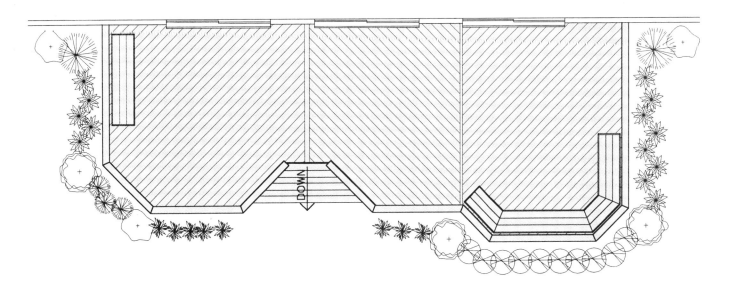

DOWN

Design HPU050070
Square Footage: 428
Width: 31'-6" Depth: 21'-0"

A large bay is perfect for an outdoor spa, with views on all sides and easy access from a short set of stairs. Spacious accommodations leave the imagination to wander over garden parties, relaxation, sunbathing and the simple pleasure of enjoying a meal outdoors.

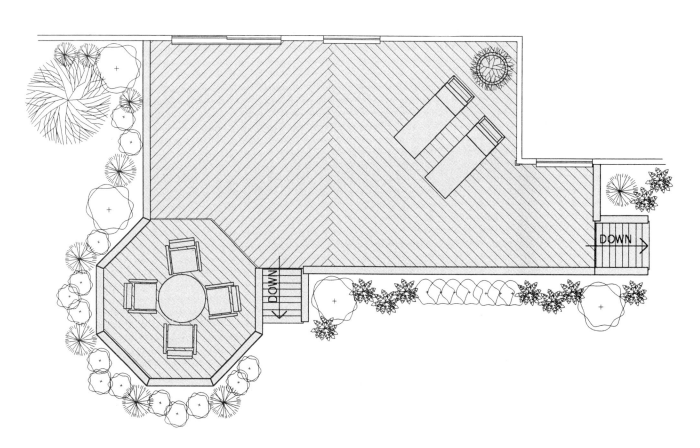

Design HPU050071

Square Footage: 449
Width: 36'-6" Depth: 12'-0"

*D*istinct areas offer ideal dining, lounging and entertaining space. With an octagonal dining bay, meals are graced with a view. A long footprint provides stairs to the yard and a step up to a patio area.

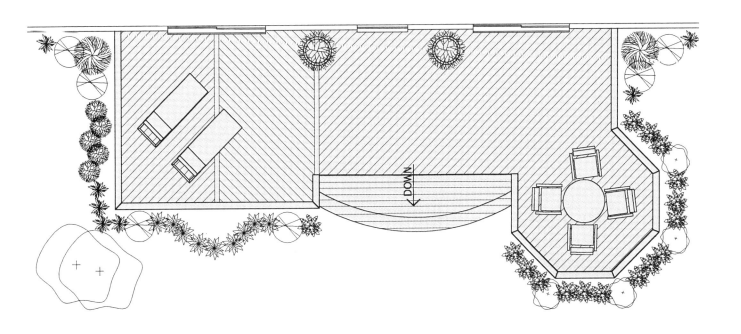

Design HPU050072

Square Footage: 464
Width: 32'-0" Depth: 15'-0"

A surprising amount of recreation space is offered with this design. There is room for alfresco dining, garden entertaining, a barbecue and open-air kitchen possibilities as well. The varying lines make a stylish statement and complement a mature landscape.

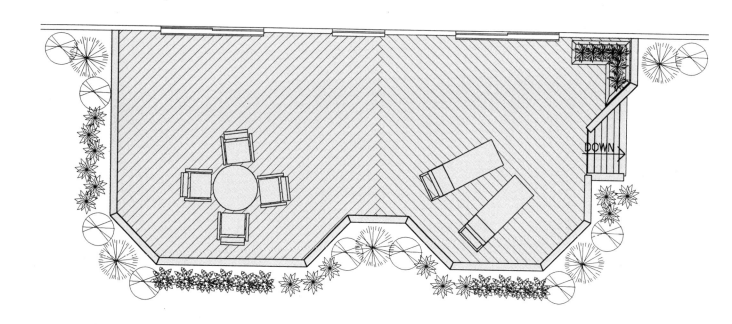

Design HPU050073
Square Footage: 479
Width: 24'-0" Depth: 22'-0"

A short stairway leads to spacious, multi-use deck space. A bumped-out bay provides for dining alfresco on warm evenings. Entertaining a crowd is easy with plenty of room for dancing, dining, stargazing or casual family get-togethers.

DOWN

Design HPU050074

Square Footage: 480
Width: 34'-0" Depth: 20'-0"

*T*wo sets of stairs allow foot traffic to move around the dining area without disturbing guests. With plenty of room left over for entertaining activities such as dancing, barbecuing, small parties or family get-togethers, this deck offers a perfect outdoor space.

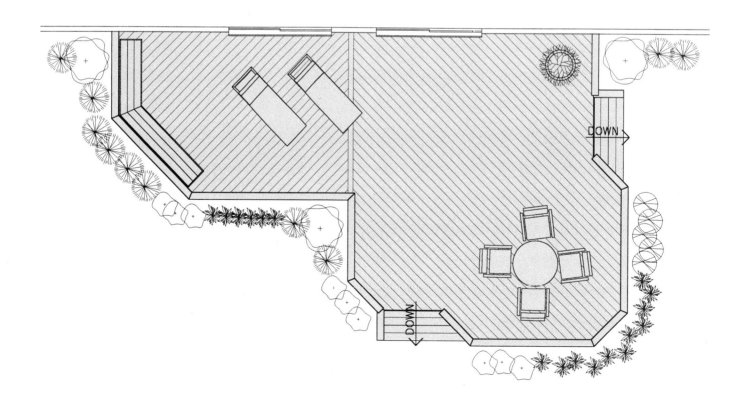

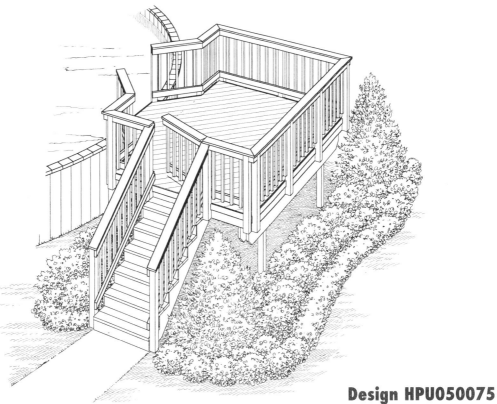

Design HPU050075
Square Footage: 98
Width: 10'-0" Depth: 11'-0"

*S*tairs lead to an entry gate that opens to a long platform. Diving space is considered with plenty of room left over for those who just want to relax.

DOWN

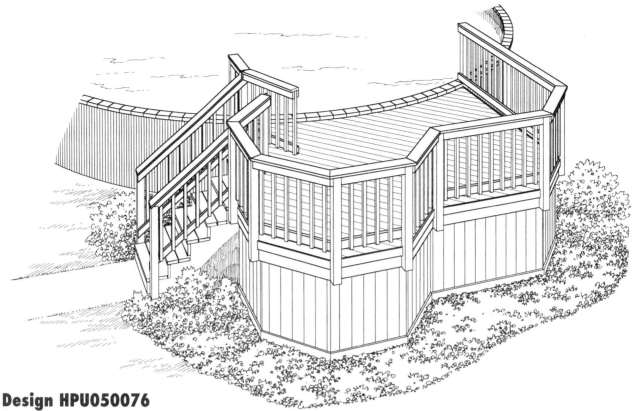

Design HPU050076
Square Footage: 129
Width: 14'-0" Depth: 12'-0"

*A*n entry gate opens to a half-octagon dining space. With a large portion of the deck set back from the poolside, entertaining guests becomes a casual affair.

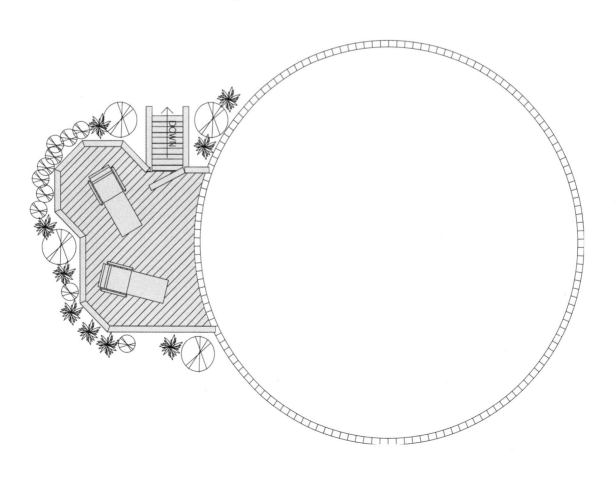

DOWN

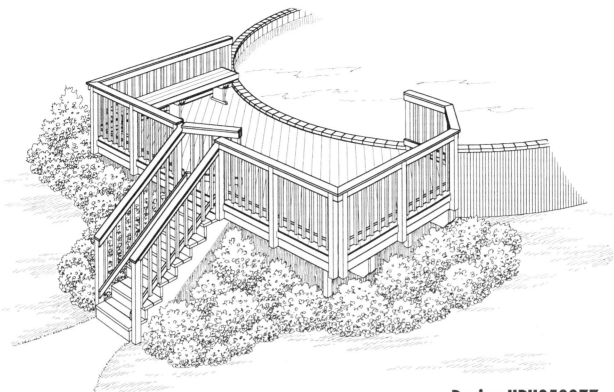

Design HPU050077

Square Footage: 166
Width: 10'-0" Depth: 24'-0"

*T*his deck features poolside lounging space with a built-in bench for keeping feet cool. With safety in mind, a gate provides a single entry to the pool deck.

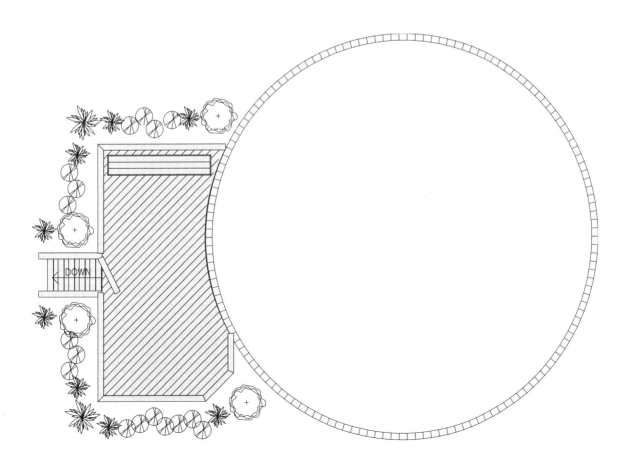

DOWN

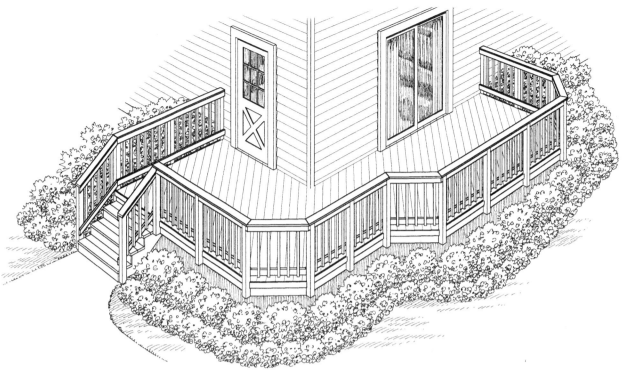

Design HPU050078

Square Footage: 234
Width: 24'-0" Depth: 16'-0"

*A*dd a beautiful twist with this modified L-shaped deck. Stair lead to the garden level from the far left, while two sides of the house enjoy access to the deck. A small cut-in to the deck lends character or conveniently avoids existing vegetation.

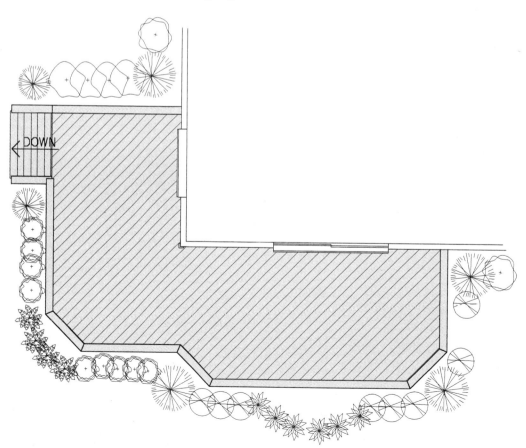

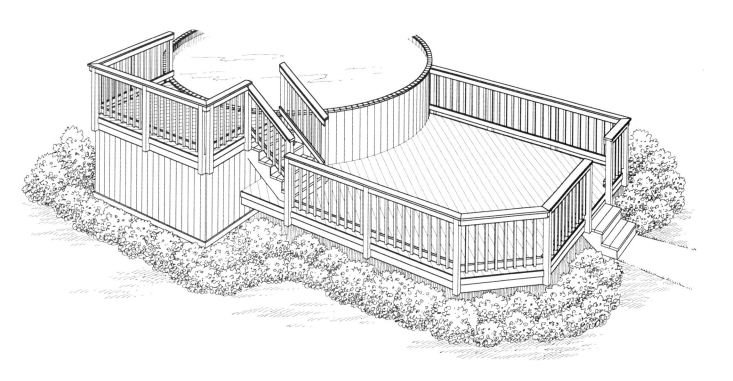

Design HPU050079
Square Footage: 256
Width: 26'-0" Depth: 18'-0"

*P*erfect *for an above-ground pool, this deck maximizes space on two levels. A small deck invites diving, while the larger area is ideal for sunning, barbecuing or relaxing near the pool.*

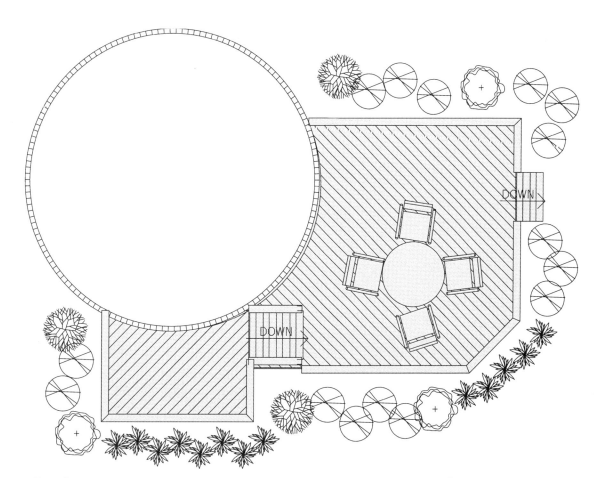

DOWN

DOWN

Design HPU050080
Square Footage: 260
Width: 20'-0" Depth: 20'-0"

*W*ith an L-shaped design, this deck is perfect for a house with rear elevation angles. Enter the deck from three different walls and enjoy the interposed curve, which will avoid large established trees or provide a creative garden design just beyond the deck area.

DOWN

Design HPU050081
Square Footage: 310
Width: 22'-0" Depth: 22'-0"

*T*he V-shaped stairs to the garden level creates two three-sided alcoves on this design. The wraparound design allows access from two sides of the home to the deck.

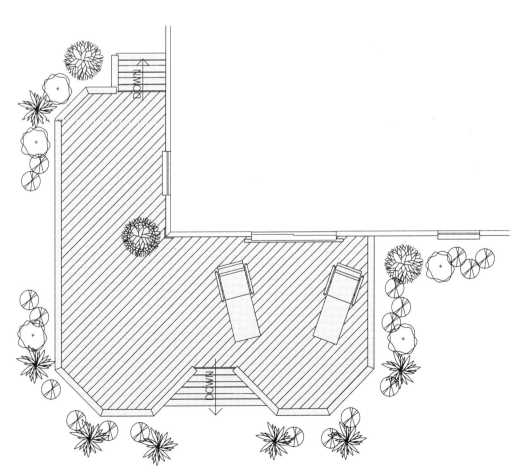

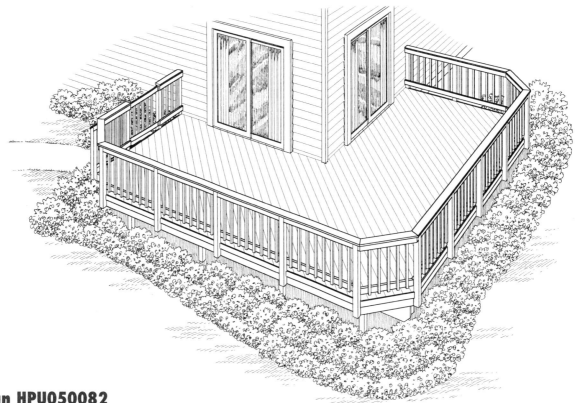

Design HPU050082

Square Footage: 334
Width: 22'-0" Depth: 22'-0"

A wraparound deck adds outdoor livability to two sides of any home! This plan offers a set of steps to the garden level from the left side of the deck.

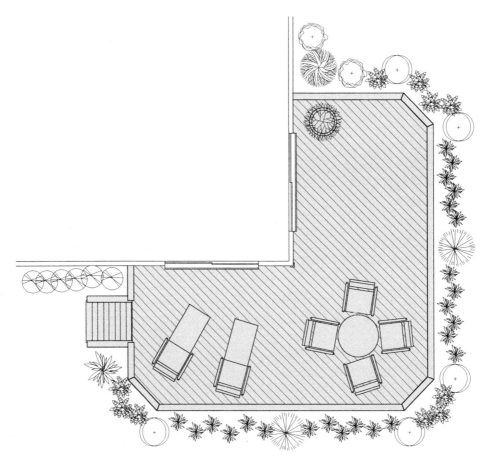

Design HPU050083

Square Footage: 336
Width: 30'-0" Depth: 17'-0"

*T*his wonderful L-shaped deck has room for multiple purposes. An alcove to the right is perfect for a table, the roomy area to the left can fit multiple chairs and a barbecue grill, and the nook to the upper right could be a small flowering plant display area.

Design HPU050084

Square Footage: 354
Width: 28'-0" Depth: 17'-0"

*A*n L-shaped bench accents one side of this wraparound deck. The illusion of separate rooms is created by a single step up from the right to the left side of the deck.

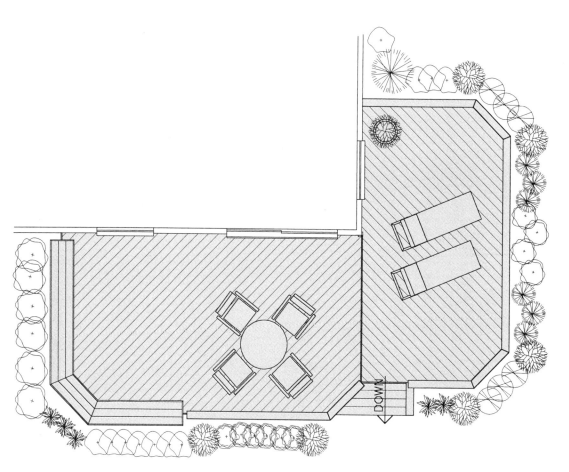

Design HPU050085

Square Footage: 354
Width: 29'-0" Depth: 23'-0"

*T*wo distinct rooms are created with box steps connecting the sides of this wraparound deck. A bench adorns the lower level, which accesses the yard.

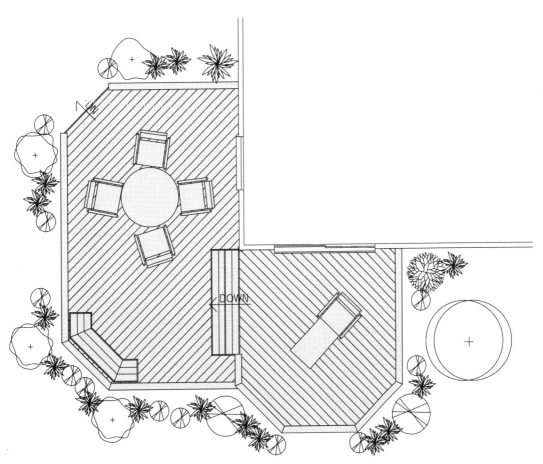

DOWN

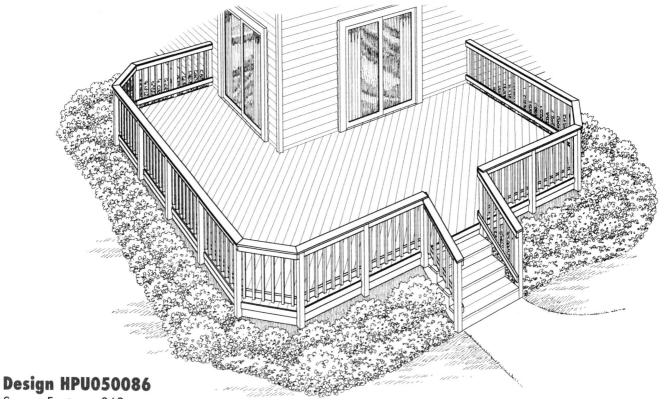

Design HPU050086

Square Footage: 362
Width: 24'-0" Depth: 22'-0"

*T*his deck allows access from two doors of the house by wrapping around a corner. One side has twelve feet of distance from the house, while the other has eight feet. Note the stairs to the garden level at the center of the main section.

Design HPU050087

Square Footage: 379
Width: 29'-0" Depth: 19'-0"

*T*his deck has many attractive angles to enhance your home. The wrap-
*around design allows access to and views of the deck via two sides. The
plan also features two sets of steps to ground level, a floating bench and flooring
set at a right angle.*

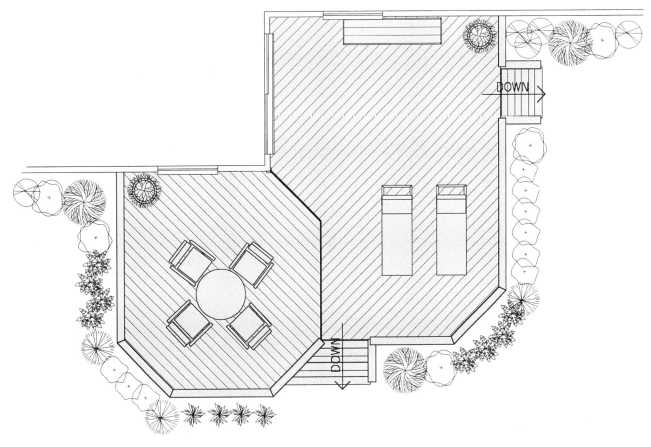

DOWN

DOWN

Design HPU050088
Square Footage: 811
Width: 40'-0" Depth: 28'-0"

This deck is a perfect start to hours of outdoor entertainment. Note the picnic table alcove to the left and the expansive deck that wraps around two sides of your home—great for lounge chairs or leave it open for social interaction.

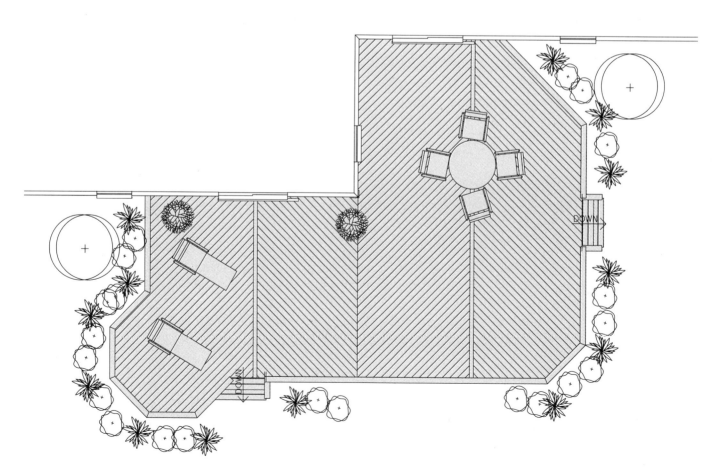

Design HPU050089
Square Footage: 226
Width: 22'-0" Depth: 12'-0"

*T*his deck is designed to fit around a bay window and could provide access *from both levels into the house. A set of stairs leads from the garden level to the lower platform. An optional floating bench can be placed on the upper section, just one step up.*

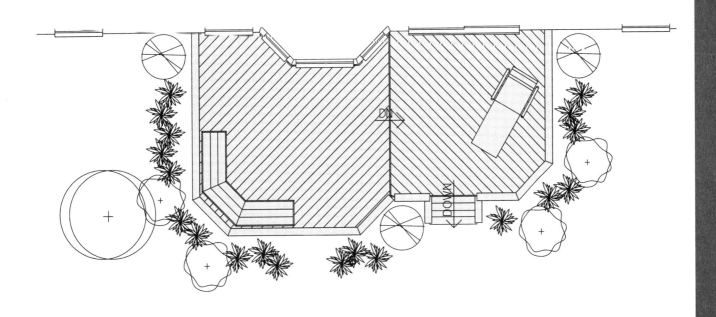

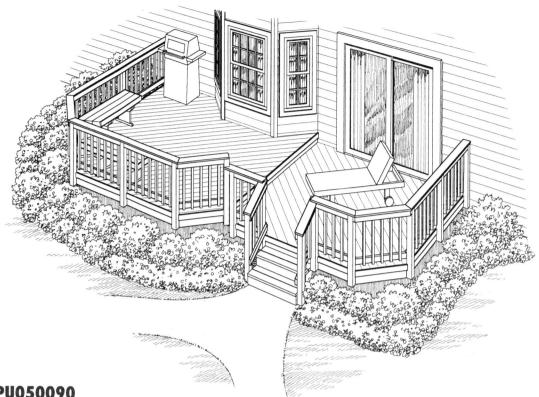

Design HPU050090
Square Footage: 238
Width: 22'-0" Depth: 12'-0"

*D*esigned to accommodate a bay window, this deck also features two levels
and an optional freestanding bench. Stairs lead to the garden level
from the lower right section.

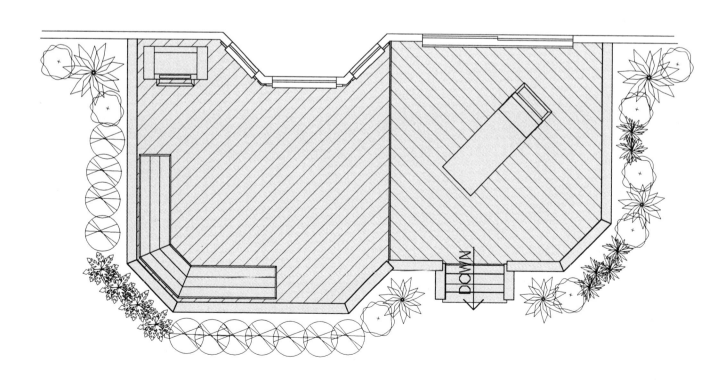

Design HPU050091
Square Footage: 246
Width: 18'-6" Depth: 16'-6"

It's hip to be square! This deck design enjoys an octagonal twist—perfect as a dining bay or spa retreat. The first level has plenty of room for a grilling area, extra seating and stairs to the rest of the yard.

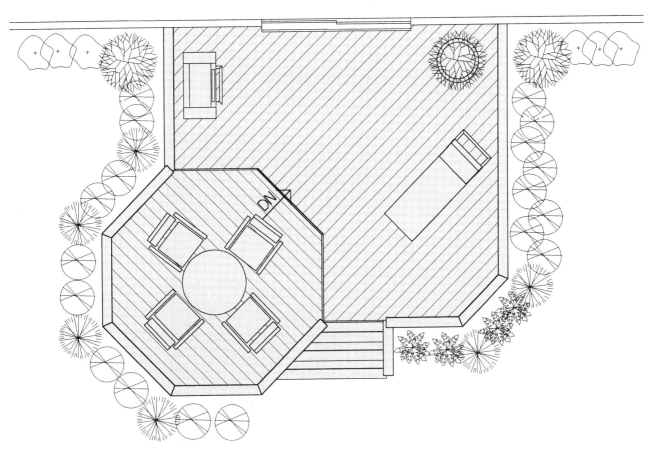

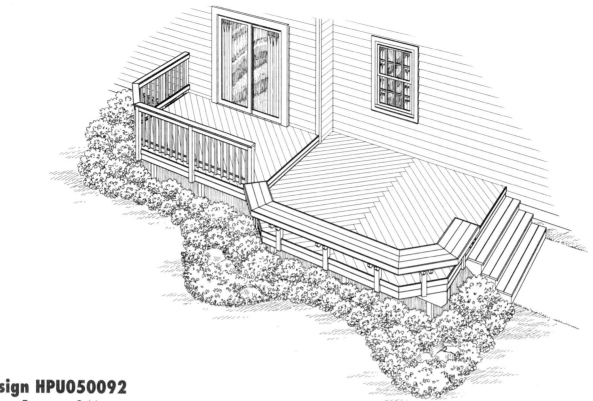

Design HPU050092

Square Footage: 246
Width: 25'-0" Depth: 12'-0"

This two-level deck accommodates a house with a two-foot change in depth. The upper deck steps down to a platform with diagonal flooring, a curved floating bench and box steps to the garden level.

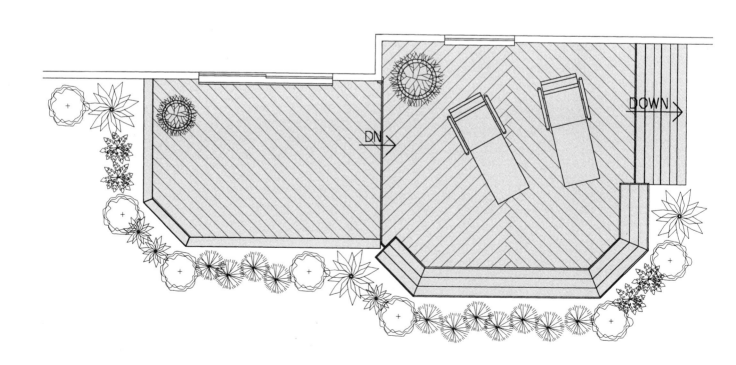

Design HPU050093
Square Footage: 256
Width: 20'-0" Depth: 14'-0"

*T*wo rectangular platforms, a shallow lower level and stairs to the yard are the simple and attractive features of this deck design. Set up a patio table and chairs for comfortable get-togethers or casual meals with a great view of your yard to offer a great backdrop.

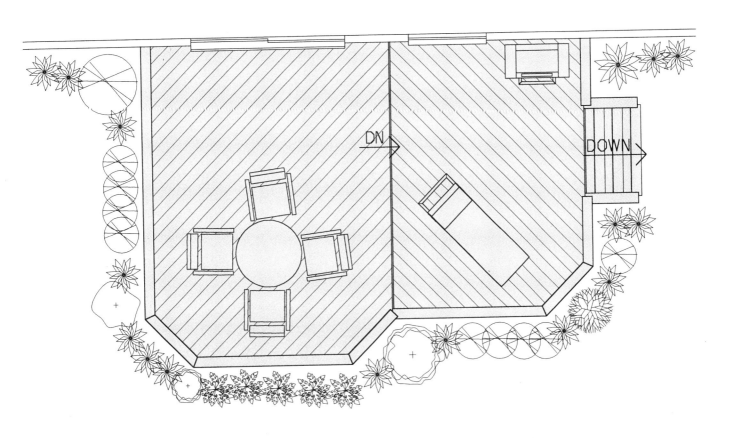

Design HPU050094
Square Footage: 264
Width: 25'-0" Depth: 12'-0"

This deck accommodates a yard with a close fit to the left ground level. Just two steps up from the garden level on the left, the sitting area of this lovely deck welcomes guests. Two more steps lead to the main platform and its eye-catching diagonal flooring.

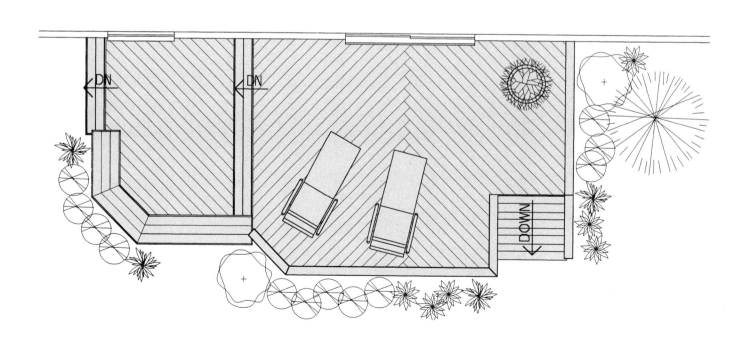

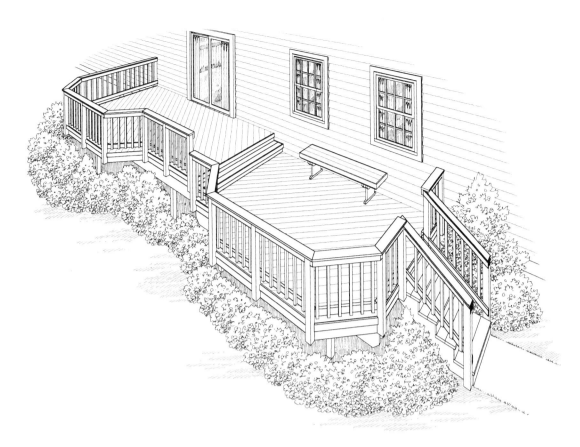

Design HPU050095

Square Footage: 285
Width: 31'-0" Depth: 10'-0"

*T*his deck will extend a full thirty-one feet along your house. The two sections are connected by a two-step elevation change. The lower platform features a freestanding bench and a set of stairs to the right.

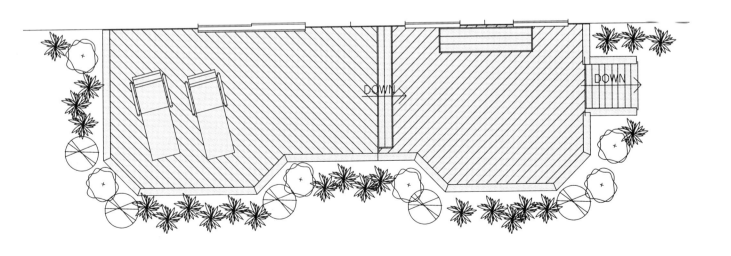

Design HPU050096

Square Footage: 296
Width: 28'-0" Depth: 14'-0"

*T*wo levels add dimension to this roomy deck. An eight-sided platform to the right features rail planters and a higher vantage point. The spacious main deck features stairs leading directly down to the ground level.

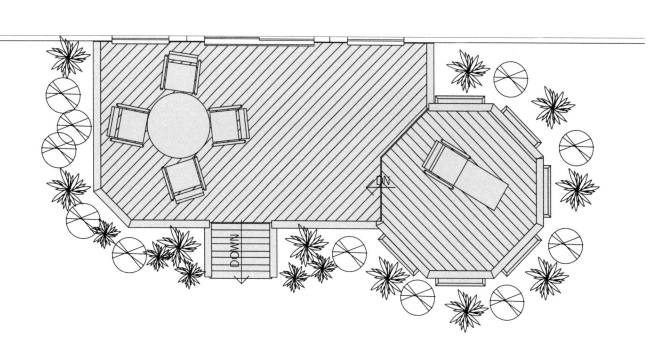

Design HPU050097
Square Footage: 296
Width: 25'-0" Depth: 14'-0"

*T*wo steps between sections of this deck create the illusion of separate rooms. The upper level features a safety rail, while the open lower level has a set of benches and two steps to the ground level.

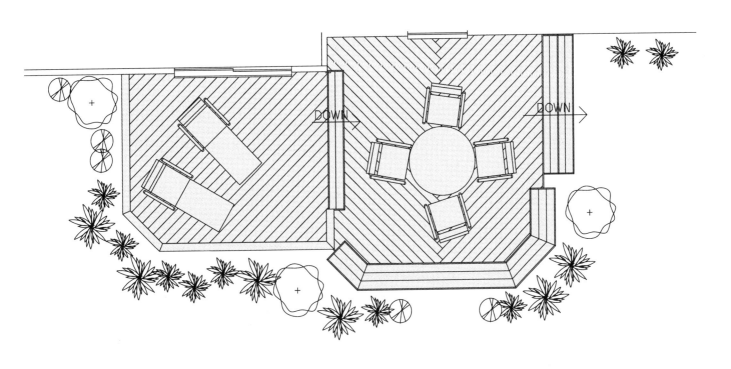

Design HPU050098

Square Footage: 300
Width: 27'-0" Depth: 15'-0"

*T*his charming two-level deck is designed to fit close to the garden level. Note the three angled stairs to the ground level—a perfect spot for potted plants adorning the sides.

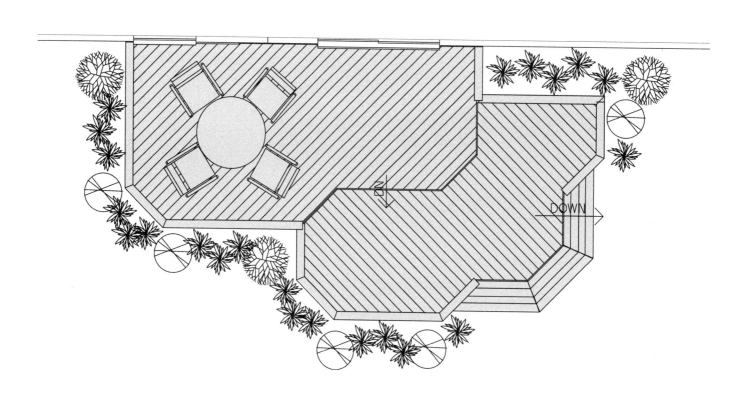

DOWN →

Design HPU050099

Square Footage: 305
Width: 27'-0" Depth: 15'-0"

A wide rectangular shape with a step up to the octagonal spa or dining bay really make this deck plan work for a larger backyard. Enjoy the extra living space with a grilling station, lounge furniture and the beauty of a potted garden while taking pleasure in the view.

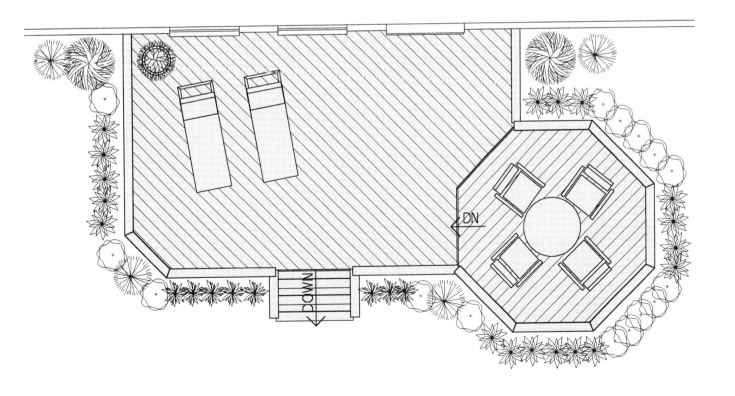

Design HPU050100

Square Footage: 306
Width: 28'-0" Depth: 12'-0"

*A*ngled box steps lead from the garden level to the lower platform on this roomy deck. A step and diagonal flooring distinguish the lower and upper levels. Lounging, grilling and entertaining are all easily possible with this design.

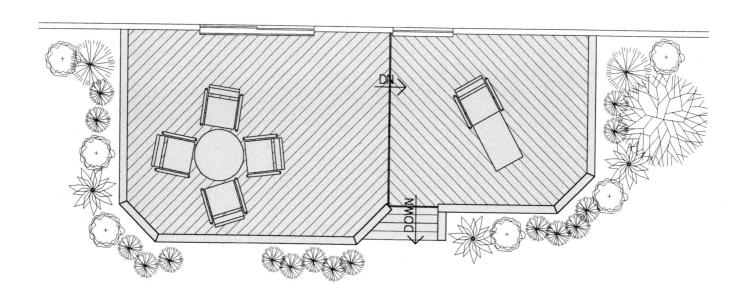

Design HPU050101

Square Footage: 314
Width: 27'-0" Depth: 19'-0"

*D*iagonal flooring and a raised observation area to the right add to the
character of this sizable deck. Note the two sets of stairs leading to the
garden level.

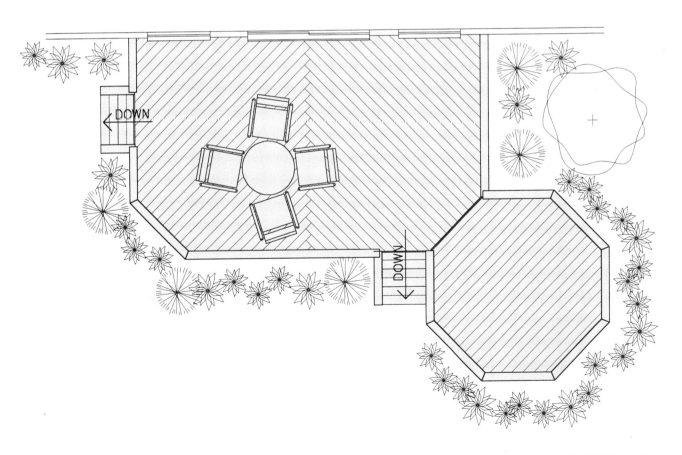

Design HPU050102

Square Footage: 320
Width: 25'-0" Depth: 18'-0"

*A*n eight-sided platform just one step above the main deck adds excitement to this design. Two benches will invite guests to rest and contemplate the outdoor vistas.

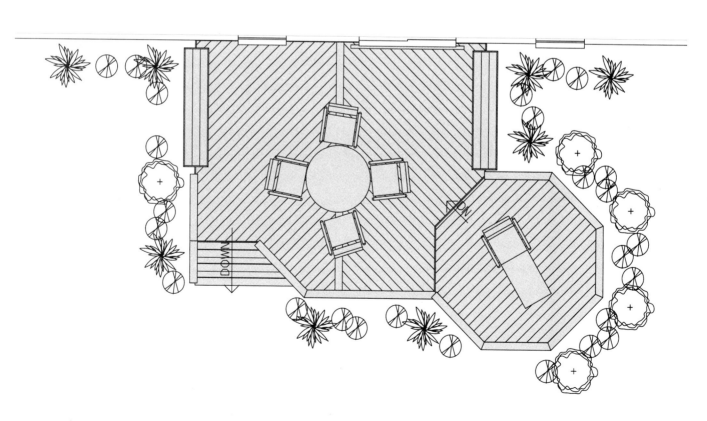

Design HPU050103
Square Footage: 322
Width: 23'-0" Depth: 20'-0"

*S*unday brunch will be an event to remember on this beautiful deck. Designed with a right-angle emphasis, the main platform has stairs to the garden level, and the upper platform can serve as a dining area.

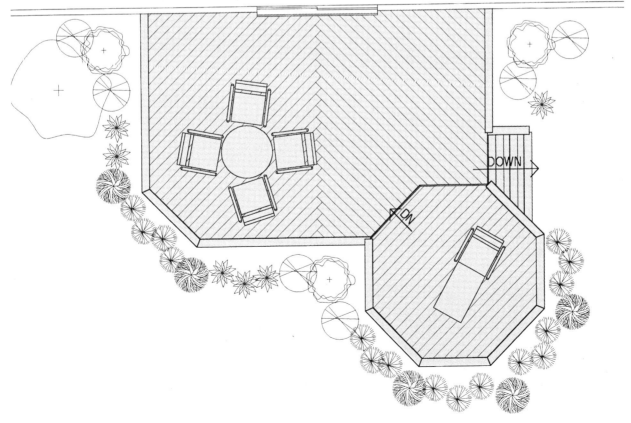

Design HPU050104

Square Footage: 345
Width: 25' Depth: 21'

*T*his deck showcases a left-angle emphasis and is perfect for lots with a view in that direction. The main platform has stairs to the garden level and also steps down to a lower observation section, which features a safety railing.

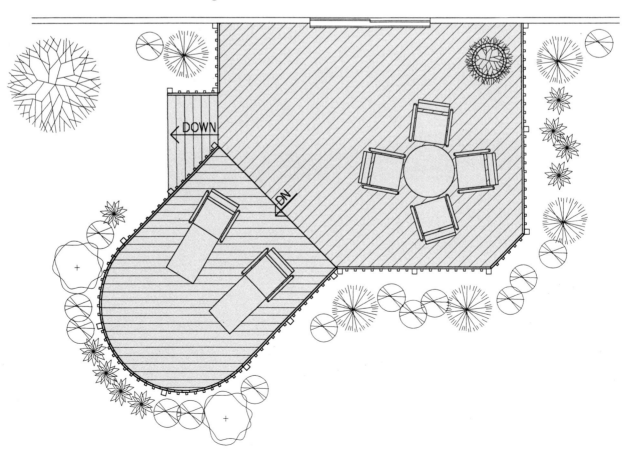

DOWN

DN

Design HPU050105

Square Footage: 323
Width: 25'-0" Depth: 15'-0"

*T*he lower level of this deck is lined with floating benches and no railing, while the upper level features a railing, an alcove and a set of stairs to the ground level.

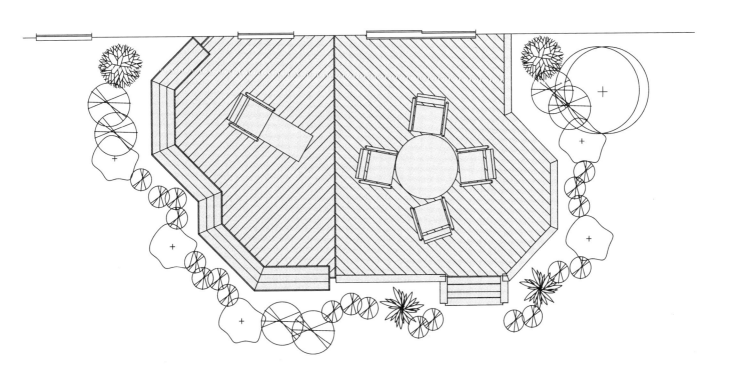

Design HPU050106
Square Footage: 325
Width: 21'-0" Depth: 18'-0"

*T*he octagonal, raised observation area is easily accessed from the main deck. Note the angled box stairs from the front of the platform to the garden level—a perfect place for potted plants.

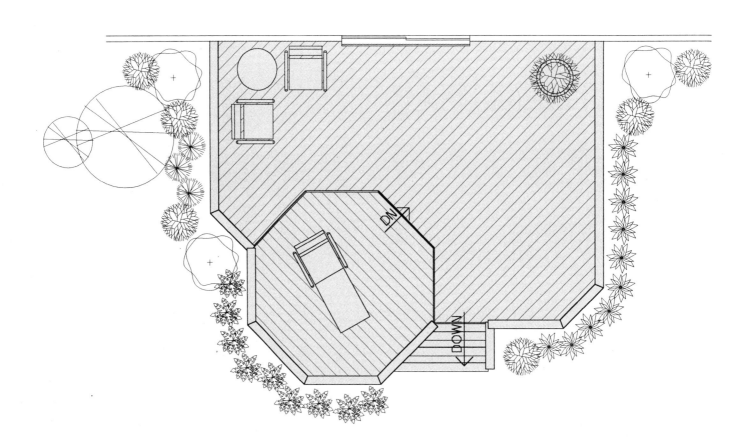

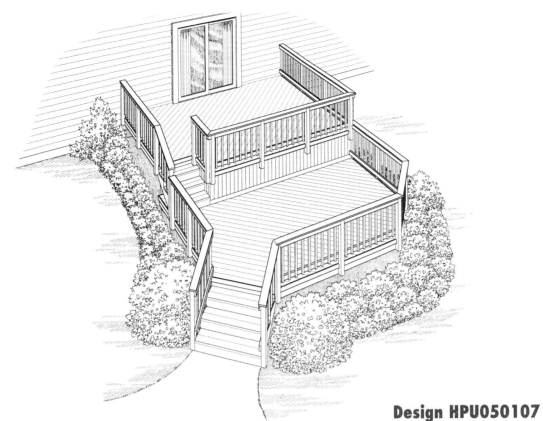

Design HPU050107
Square Footage: 343
Width: 16'-0" Depth: 22'-0"

This design creates two deck spaces on a sloping lot. The upper platform allows access to the house and has a flight of stairs and a safety railing separating it from the lower deck. A second flight of stairs leads from the lower section to the garden level.

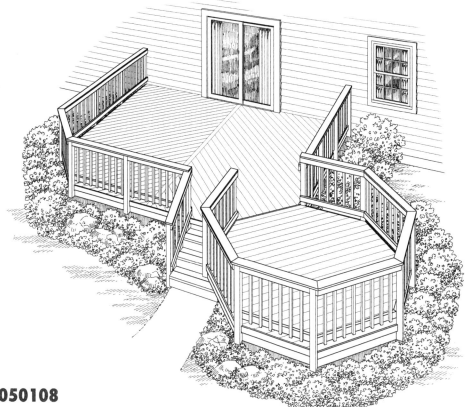

Design HPU050108

Square Footage: 343
Width: 25'-0" Depth: 22'-0"

*G*et outdoors on this beautiful deck. Diagonal flooring and an octagonal dining area—set a step above the main floor—make this a charming retreat.

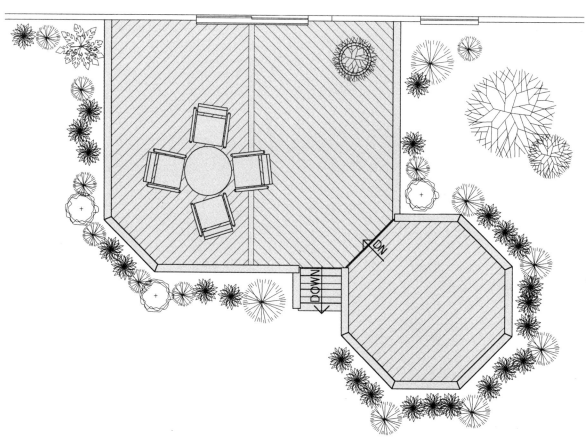

DOWN

Design HPU050109

Square Footage: 347
Width: 25'-0" Depth: 15'-0"

*E*njoy the feel of the great outdoors from the safety of this charming deck. Two floating benches enhance the design, which includes two levels and a bayed alcove on the upper level.

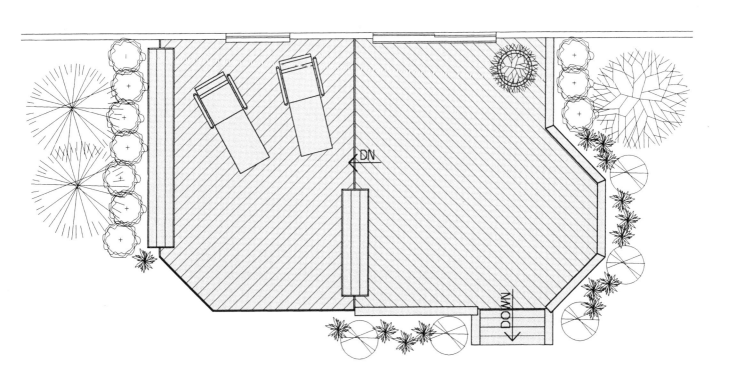

Design HPU050110

Square Footage: 352
Width: 28'-0" Depth: 15'-0"

Select a design to match the bay window on your house! This deck offers that and floating benches, beautifully tiered semi-circular steps to garden level, built-in planter boxes and an angled step down from the upper to lower deck level.

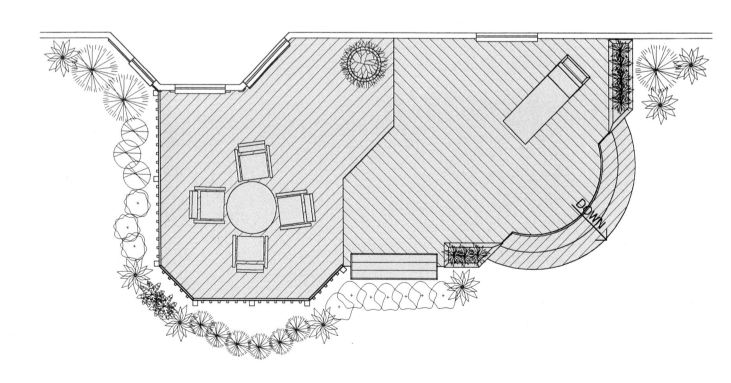

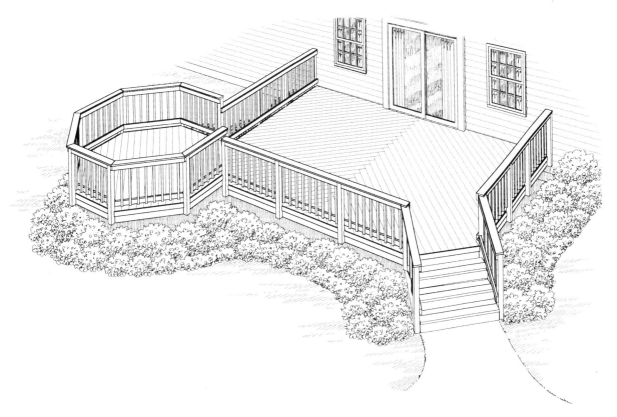

Design HPU050111
Square Footage: 374
Width: 27'-0" Depth: 22'-0"

*A*n octagon observation deck—or make it a dining area!—is set apart from the main deck via a small step in elevation. The lower section features stairs to the garden level from the right corner.

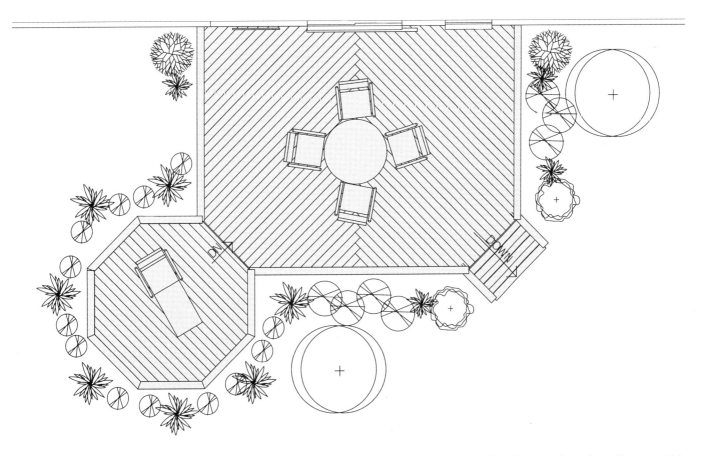

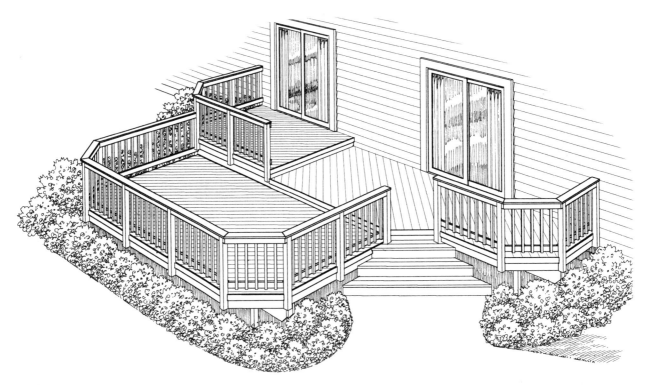

Design HPU050112

Square Footage: 385
Width: 26'-6" Depth: 18'-0"

Three levels lend appeal to this deck. Angled flooring and flared stairs add to its visual interest. With its multiple layers, this deck design holds endless entertainment possibilities.

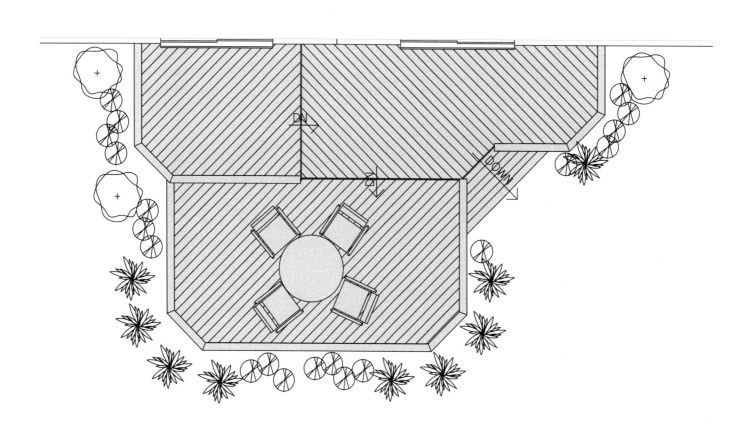

Design HPU050113
Square Footage: 389
Width: 26'-0" Depth: 19'-0"

*T*his deck will extend a full twenty-six feet along your house. Two optional, curved freestanding benches can be placed in the twin alcoves on each side of the stairs. A large platform at the end of the stairs adds charm.

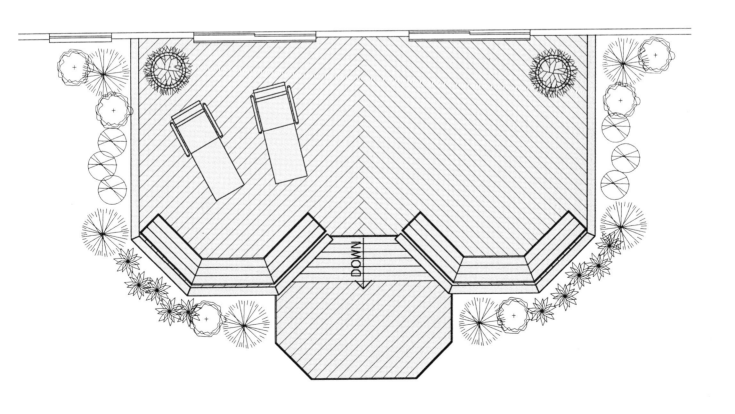

DOWN

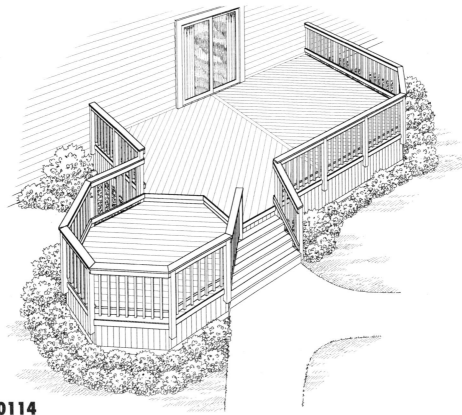

Design HPU050114

Square Footage: 391
Width: 29'-0" Depth: 18'-0"

*D*iagonal flooring adorns this deck, which adds over 390 square feet of livability to your home. A step down separates the octagonal alcove to the left of the plan from the main area.

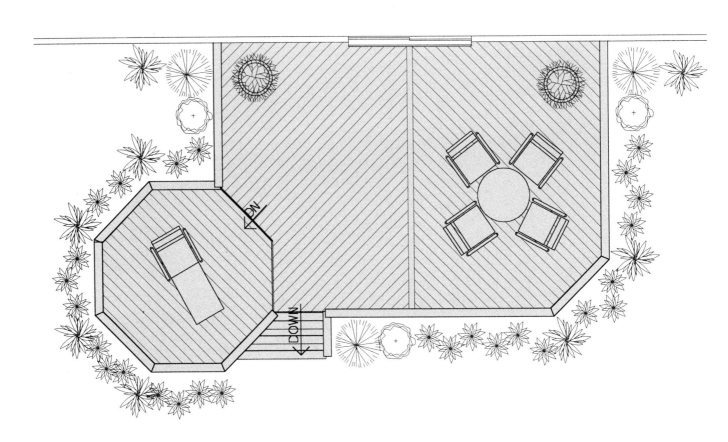

Design HPU050115

Square Footage: 392
Width: 25'-0" Depth: 22'-0"

*T*wo sets of stairs lead from the garden level to the main platform of this roomy deck. An eight-sided dining platform is just a step above and to the left, creating beauty and depth.

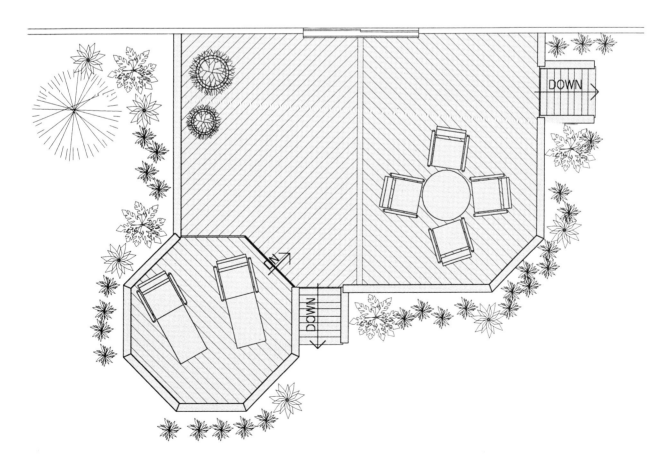

DOWN

DOWN

Design HPU050116

Square Footage: 396
Width: 24'-0" Depth: 21'-0"

Curvy shapes and inviting spaces can be found with this deck design. An optional, freestanding bench is a perfect complement to the relaxing atmosphere you are sure to enjoy. A octagonal bay will serve as either a dining alcove or spa area with a great look out spot.

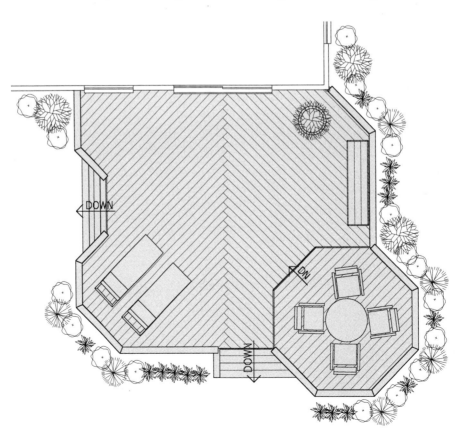

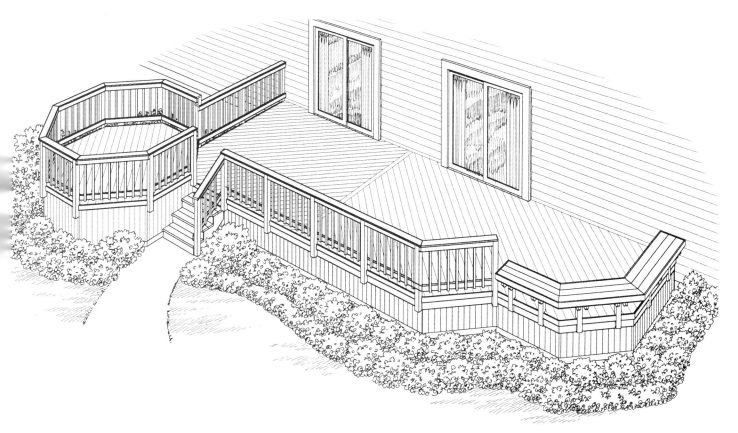

Design HPU050117
Square Footage: 433
Width: 39'-0" Depth: 19'-0"

*A*dorn your house with thirty-nine feet of exterior livability found with this deck. An eight-sided eating/observation deck is one step up from the main level. Note the floating bench to the right and the stairs beside the raised observation area.

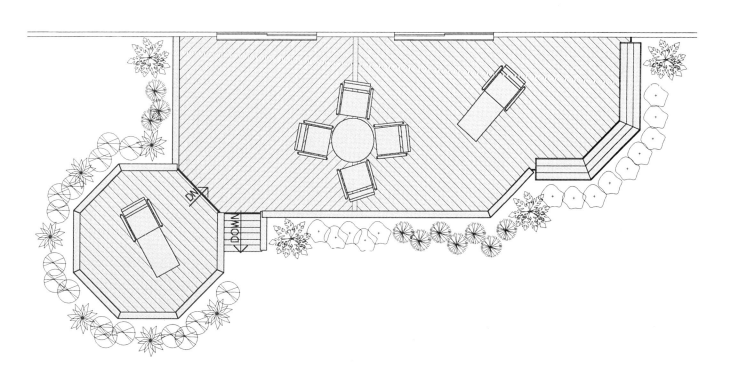

Design HPU050118

Square Footage: 433
Width: 39'-0" Depth: 13'-0"

*D*esigned to accommodate a two-foot change in elevation on the house, this deck has two sections connected by a step down, two sets of stairs to the garden level from a central location, an optional rail planter and a floating L-shaped bench.

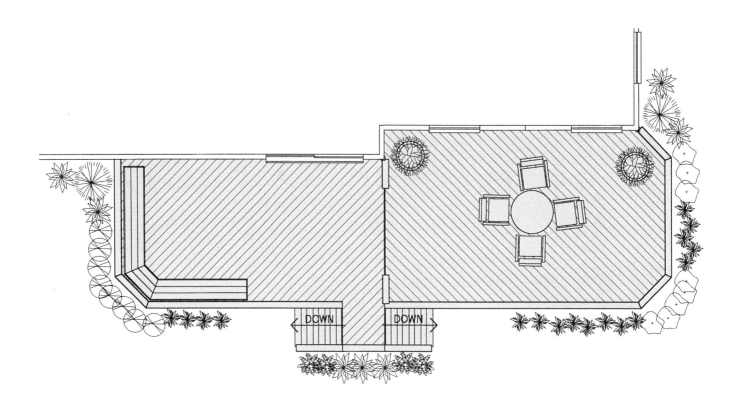

DOWN DOWN

Design HPU050119
Square Footage: 468
Width: 35'-0" Depth: 15'-0"

*M*ultiple uses abound with this thirty-five foot of deck. The main section features a diagonally set floor and has plenty of room for a grill, table and chairs. One step down, there is a platform perfect for a spa or lounge chairs.

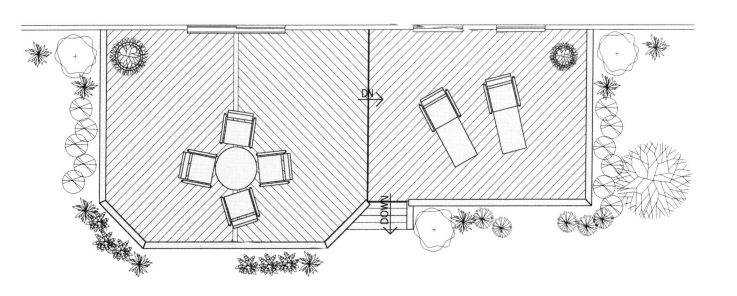

Design HPU050120

Square Footage: 476
Width: 33'-0" Depth: 22'-0"

This amazing deck features an octagonal, raised platform, perfect for a table and chairs. The area designed to attach to the house includes a floating bench and diagonal flooring.

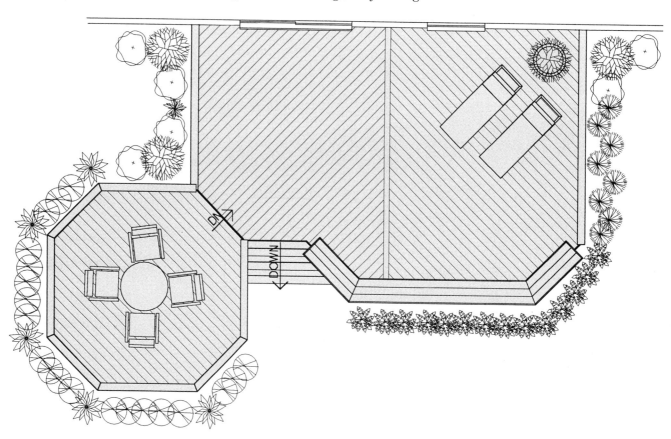

Design HPU050121
Square Footage: 483
Width: 35'-6" Depth: 19'-0"

*A*n octagonal dining platform adds charm to this three-level deck. Access the deck via one of two sections along the house. The lowest level to the right includes two steps to the ground level and an optional freestanding bench.

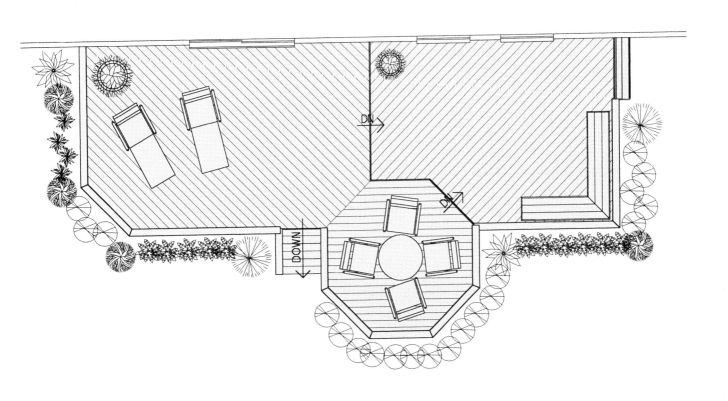

DN

DN

DOWN

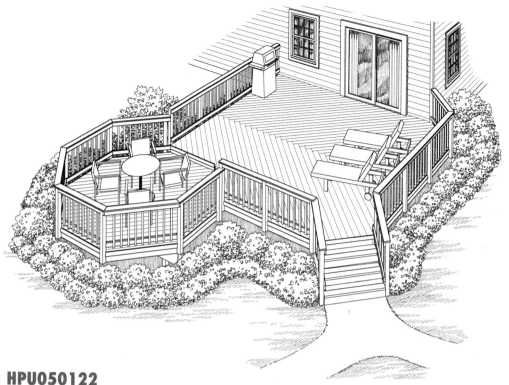

Design HPU050122

Square Footage: 487
Width: 29'-6" Depth: 25'-6"

Diagonal flooring enhances the appearance of this roomy deck. A dining platform is set off by an octagon shape and is one step lower than the main section. Note the stairs leading from the right corner of the design.

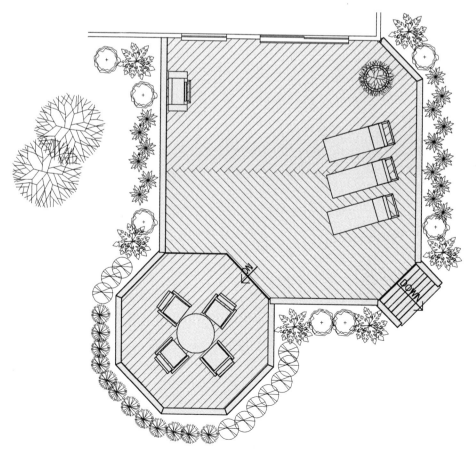

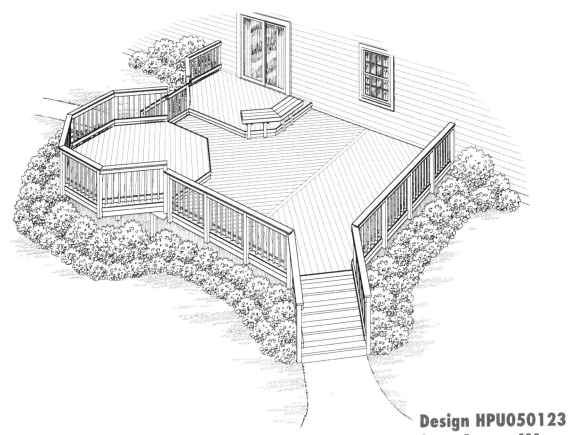

Design HPU050123

Square Footage: 538
Width: 27'-0" Depth: 23'-6"

A cozy platform with a floating bench accesses the house, while one step down on either side is the largest section of this deck. One step up to the left is an octagonal dining platform, making outdoor entertainment a breeze. Two sets of stairs access the garden level.

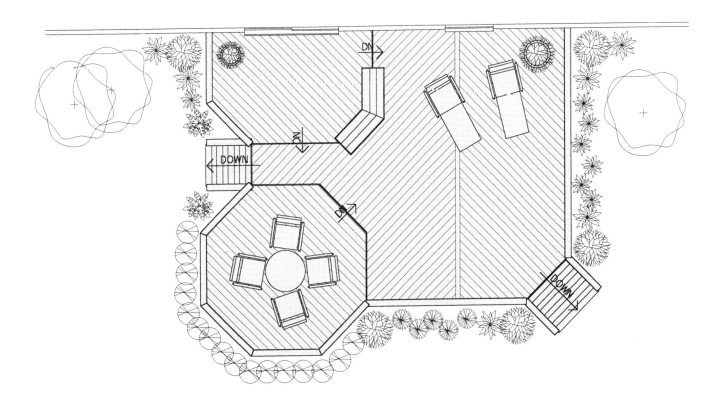

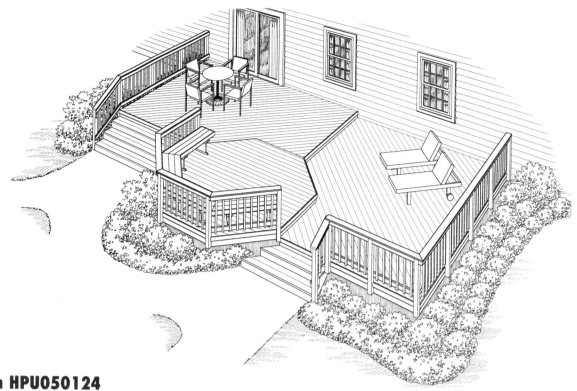

Design HPU050124

Square Footage: 574
Width: 33'-0" Depth: 21'-6"

*A*n octagonal observation platform sits front and center on this deck. To the left, lengthy box steps lead to the garden level and provide a great display location for flowering plants. Create the illusion of a separate deck with the lower section, just one step down to the right.

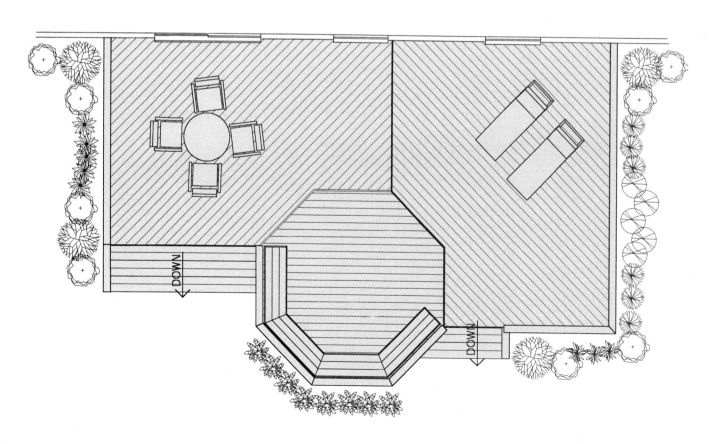

Design HPU050125

Square Footage: 634
Width: 46'-0" Depth: 15'-0"

*E*xtend *your outdoor living by forty-six feet with this deck. One step down to the left is a roomy platform for dining, a spa or a grill. Flowerpots would beautify the boxed steps to the garden level.*

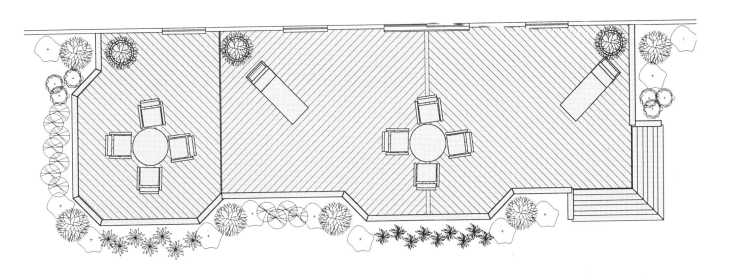

Design HPU050126

Square Footage: 658
Width: 43'-0" Depth: 22'-0"

*E*xtended outdoor living has never offered so much! Two octagonal alcoves adorn this plan. One is set one step above the main platform and would be a perfect outdoor dining area. Enhance your deck further with optional freestanding benches.

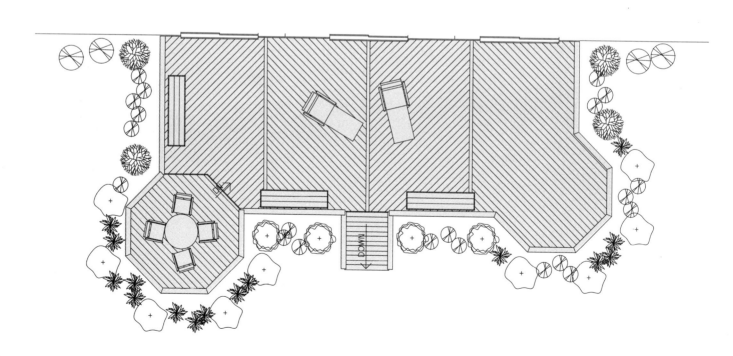

DOWN

Design HPU050127
Square Footage: 727
Width: 40'-0" Depth: 25'-0"

*T*his deck has something to please any outdoor enthusiast. An octagonal section enjoys a freestanding bench and is two steps down from the main platform. Diagonal flooring enhances the main area, while another freestanding bench and curved steps add to the perfection.

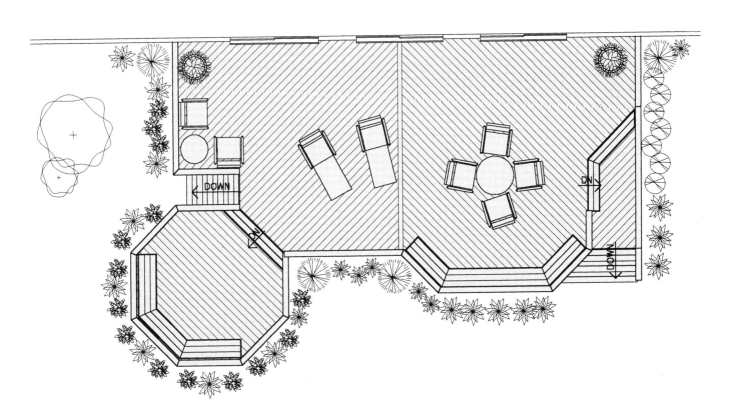

The Deck Blueprint Package

OUR PLANS AND DETAILS ARE CAREFULLY PREPARED in an easy-to-understand format that will guide you through every stage of your deck-building project. The Deck Blueprint Package contains numerous sheets outlining information pertinent to the specific Deck Plan you have chosen. A separate package—Deck Accessory Construction Details—provides the how-to data for building benches, planters and a freestanding buffet.

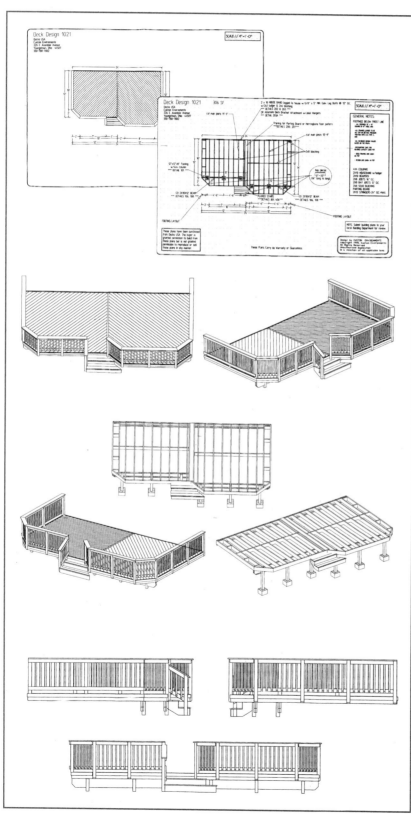

CUSTOM DECK PLANS

Each deck plan shown on pages 13 to 139 has been custom designed. With each custom deck plan, you receive the following:

DECK FRAMING AND FLOOR PLANS

In clear, easy-to-read drawings, these sheets shows all component parts of the deck from an aerial viewpoint with dimensions, notes and references. Drawn at 1/4" = 1'-0", the floor plan provides a finished overhead view of the deck. The framing plan gives complete details on how the deck is to be built, including the position and spacing of footings, joists, beams, posts and decking materials.

3-D STRUCTURE AND RENDERED VIEWS

An artist's 3-D line drawing shows the deck when completed. This drawing provides a visual image of structural elements, plus rails, stairs and other details of the deck.

DECK ELEVATIONS

Large-scale front and side elevations complete the visual picture of the deck. The elevations illustrate the height of rails, balusters, stair risers, benches and other deck accessories.

DECK MATERIALS LIST AND MATERIALS TAKE-OFF

This shopping list includes the basic materials needed (including sizes and amounts) to build your deck. The materials list is complemented by detail drawings showing placement of hardware such as thru-bolts, screws, nuts, washers and nails and how these items are used to secure deck flooring, rails, posts and joists. The materials take-off provides a handy shopping list that consolidates the many pieces of the materials list for easier ordering.

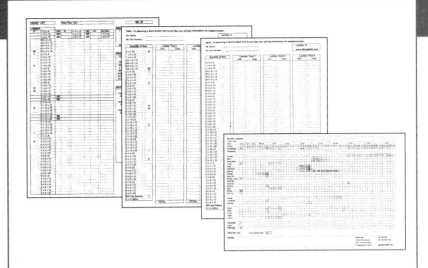

DECK CONSTRUCTION DETAILS

The Deck Construction Details package outlines basic steps in the construction of common elements of decks, showing items such as a typical deck section, a deck anatomy, footings, house band attachment, column notches and other important framing and decking details. The information applies to the building of any deck and will be extremely helpful in understanding the deck building process.

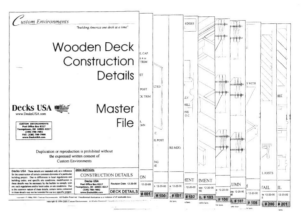

STAIR CONSTRUCTION DETAILS

To help with one of the most difficult aspects of deck building, the Stair Construction Details gives important information for planning stairs in the project and then constructing them so they are safe. Filled with drawings showing how to construct stringer stairs, flared stairs, box steps and various railings, this packet of details will be invaluable for the do-it-yourselfer. There's even a handy chart which outlines how many steps you'll need and what the measurements of the risers and bottom should be.

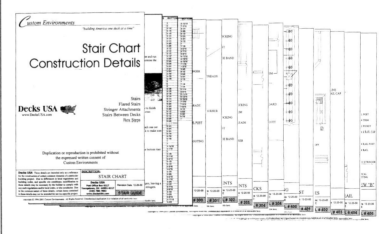

DECK ACCESSORY CONSTRUCTION DETAILS

To make your deck even more useful and dramatic, the Deck Accessory Construction Details packages (sold separately at $2.95 each) include building information for different types of benches, two planter versions and a freestanding buffet. Showing dimensions for top and side views of these additions, the Accessory Details kits help you transform your deck from plain and simple to a true outdoor design statement.

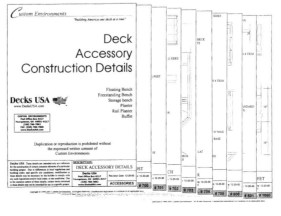

Deck Plan Prices and Index

CUSTOM DECK PLANS

PRICES GUARANTEED THROUGH DECEMBER 31, 2001

1-SET STUDY PACKAGE	4-SET BUILDING PACKAGE	8-SET BUILDING PACKAGE	1-SET REPRODUCIBLES
$40	$70	$110	$160

OPTIONS:

ADDITIONAL IDENTICAL BLUEPRINTS IN SAME ORDER ....$10 PER SET
REVERSE BLUEPRINTS (MIRROR IMAGE) WITH 4- OR 8-SET ORDER ....$10 FEE
DECK ACCESSORY CONSTRUCTION DETAILS...$2.95 FOR EACH:
FLOATING BENCH • STORAGE BENCH • PLANTER • RAIL PLANTER • FREESTANDING BUFFET

PLAN INDEX

To Order:

CHOOSE YOUR FAVORITE DECK PLAN and then determine if you will need the 1-set Study Package, the 4-set or 8-set Building Package or the 1-set Reproducibles Package, adding any additional or reverse sets you desire. The Deck Accessory Construction Details package is sold separately, and offers a wealth of information for making your deck even more usable. Please call our toll free number to place your order 1-866-335-2665. If you prefer to use our order form, please call our toll-free number for current pricing and availability.

OUR SERVICE POLICY
We try to process and ship every order from our office within two business days. For this reason, we won't send a formal notice acknowledging receipt of your order.

OUR EXCHANGE POLICY
Since blueprints are printed in response to your order, we cannot honor requests for refunds. However, we will exchange your entire first order for an equal or greater number of blueprints within our plan collection within 90 days of the original order. The entire content of your original order must be returned to our offices before an exchange will be processed. If the returned blueprints look used, redlined or copied, we will not honor your exchange. Fees for exchanging your blueprints are 20% of the amount of the original order. (Reproducible blueprints are not exchangeable or returnable.) Please add $8 for postage and handling via Regular Service; $12 via Priority Service; $22 via Express Service. Shipping and handling charges are not refundable.

ABOUT REVERSE BLUEPRINTS
If you want to install your deck in reverse of the plan as shown, we will include reversed sets of blueprints with the Framing and Floor plans and Elevations reversed for an additional fee of $10.00 for 4- or 8-set package. Although call-outs and lettering will appear backward, reverses will prove useful as a visual aid if you decide to flop the plan.

HOW MANY BLUEPRINTS DO I NEED?
Although a standard building package may satisfy many states, cities and counties, some plans may require certain changes. For your convenience, we have developed a Reproducible plan, which allows a local professional to modify and make up to 10 copies of your revised plan. As our plans are all copyright protected, with your purchase of the Reproducible, we will supply you with a copyright release letter. The number of copies you may need: 1 for owner, 3 for builder, 2 for local building department and 1-3 sets for your mortgage lender.

DISCLAIMER
We and the designers we work with have put substantial care and effort into the creation of our blueprints. However, because we cannot provide on-site consultation, supervision and control over actual construction, and because of the great variance in local building requirements, building practices and soil, seismic, weather and other conditions, WE CANNOT MAKE ANY WARRANTY, EXPRESS OR IMPLIED, WITH RESPECT TO THE CONTENT OR USE OF OUR BLUEPRINTS, INCLUDING, BUT NOT LIMITED TO, ANY WARRANTY OF MERCHANTABILITY OR OF FITNESS FOR A PARTICULAR PURPOSE. ITEMS, PRICES, TERMS & CONDITIONS ARE SUBJECT TO CHANGE WITHOUT NOTICE. REPRODUCIBLE PLAN ORDERS MAY REQUIRE A CUSTOMER'S SIGNED RELEASE BEFORE SHIPPING ORDER.

BLUEPRINT HOTLINE
Call Toll-Free1-866-DEKBOOK (1-866-335-2665). We'll ship your order within 2 business days if you call us by 3:00 p.m. Eastern Time. When you order by phone, please be prepared to give us the Order Form Key Number shown in the box at the bottom of the Order Form. By FAX: Copy the order form at right and send on our FAX line: 1-800-224-6699 or 520-544-3086.

CANADIAN CUSTOMERS
Order Toll-Free 1-877-223-6389

For Customer Service, Call Toll-Free 1-888-690-1116

Blueprints are not Refundable
Exchanges Only

Order Form

Call for current pricing and availability prior to mailing this order form.

Home Planners, LLC
Wholly owned by Hanley-Wood, LLC
3275 West Ina Road, Suite 110
Tucson, Arizona 85741

PLEASE RUSH ME THE FOLLOWING:
__ Set(s) of Custom Deck Plan _____ $_____
    (See Deck Plans Prices and Index)
__ Additional identical blueprints
    in same order @ $10.00 per set $_____
__ Reverse blueprints @10.00 fee (from 4 or 8 set package) $_____
__ Deck Accessory Construction Details ($2.95 each) $_____

POSTAGE AND HANDLING
Signature is required for all deliveries.

No CODs (requires street address—No P.O. Boxes)	
• Regular Service (Allow 7-10 days delivery)	$8.00
• Priority Service (Allow 4-5 days delivery)	$12.00
• Express Service (Allow 3 days delivery)	$22.00

Overseas Delivery: Fax, phone or mail for quote
Note: All delivery times are from date Blueprint Package is shipped.

Postage (From shaded box above) $_____
Subtotal $_____

Sales Tax: (AZ and MI residents please add appropriate
            state and local sales tax.) $_____

Total (subtotal and tax) $_____

Your Address (please print legibly)

Name _____

Street _____

City _____ State _____ Zip _____

Daytime telephone number (required) (____) _____

Credit Card Orders Only

Credit Card number _____

Exp. Date (M/Y) _____

Check one:
❑ Visa ❑ MasterCard ❑ Discover Card ❑ American Express

Signature (required) _____
Please check appropriate box:
❑ Licensed Builder-Contractor ❑ Homeowner

Order Toll Free!
1-866-DEKBOOK (1-866-335-2665)
BY FAX: Copy the order form above and send it
on our FAX LINE: 1-800-224-6699 or 1-520-544-3086

ORDER FORM KEY
HPU05

Notes

_____

_____

_____

_____

_____

_____

_____

_____

_____

_____

_____

_____

_____

_____

_____

_____

_____